Petrus Johannes Beckx, Edward Hazeland

Month of Mary

Petrus Johannes Beckx, Edward Hazeland

Month of Mary

ISBN/EAN: 9783742858924

Manufactured in Europe, USA, Canada, Australia, Japa

Cover: Foto ©Lupo / pixelio.de

Manufactured and distributed by brebook publishing software (www.brebook.com)

Petrus Johannes Beckx, Edward Hazeland

Month of Mary

MONTH OF MARY.

BY THE

Very Rev. FATHER BECKX,
GENERAL OF THE SOCIETY OF JESUS.

Translated from the German by
Mrs. EDWARD HAZELAND.

BURNS AND OATES,

LONDON :	NEW YORK :
GRANVILLE MANSIONS	CATHOLIC PUBLICATION SOCIETY CO.
ORCHARD STREET. W.	BARCLAY STREET.

Nihil Obstat.

GEORGIUS PORTER, SOC. JES.,
Censor deputatus.

Imprimatur.

HENRICUS EDUARDUS,
CARD. ARCHIEP. WESTMONAST.

Die 17 Aprilis, 1884.

PREFACE TO THE 14TH EDITION.

THIS little manual was first published in Vienna, in the year 1838. The numerous editions already issued testify to its worth, as also do the Italian, Polish, and Dutch translations of the same. For some time the German edition was out of print, and although several other Months of Mary had been given to the public, they did not quench the wide-spread desire that a new edition of this work should be printed. With this desire the venerable author most readily complied, and it is hoped that this little manual, which has already been so efficacious in furthering devotion to our Blessed Lady, may prove an acceptable gift to all her devout clients.

Feast of St. Joseph, 1880.

My Dear Mrs. Hazeland,

Our Very Rev. Father General, Father Beckx, willingly consents to your translating his "Month of Mary" into English. He has given me a copy of the latest German edition for you, and I forward it by this post.

I hope the book will meet the same kindly reception in its English dress which the original German and the Italian edition have had.

I remain,

Yours very truly,

GEORGE PORTER.

San Girolamo,
 Fiesole, *June 21, 1883.*

INTRODUCTION.

A few remarks concerning the aim of this work.

THE same spirit of devotion which led to the recitation of the Angelic Salutation, thrice daily, in Mary's honour, and to the setting apart Saturday for the same purpose, has also prompted the faithful to dedicate one month of the year to the Divine Mother. May was selected, because this month, the most lovely of the whole year, seemed most befitting the Mother of Perfect Love; also, to counteract the innate thirst for pleasure and light-heartedness so natural in this month, and which, if indulged to the full, leads often to such sad results. It was therefore deemed wise to use every effort to turn such feelings in a right direction, and tune the sinner's lips to hymn the Virgin's praise.

INTRODUCTION.

This devotion had its origin in Rome* and is now observed in many Churches, with the utmost pomp, and with sermon and benediction daily. No year passes without abundant proofs of the numerous graces and blessings obtained by Mary's intercession for those who render her special honour through this month. From Rome, this practice extended to other provinces and countries. Many works were written

---

* Isolated traces of special devotion to Mary during the month of May are to be met with in the earlier ages of the Church's history. Henry Suso relates how he set apart the 1st of May in honour of the Blessed Virgin, in order to make some amends for the forgetfulness evinced her at this time by the pleasure-loving votaries of the world. St. Philip Neri was accustomed to incite the young people under his guidance to pay special homage to Mary during this month, so full of danger for their innocence. Father Francis Salomia is accredited with being the founder of the devotions of the month of May, as now practised. He first introduced this devotion among the youthful members of the Confraternity of Mary who were under his care, and compiled a manual for their use. The May devotions have spread with wonderful rapidity since Pope Pius

in order to aid its extension, and amongst others, the present manual, in the German tongue. It contains a meditation for each day, a prayer from the Litany of Loretto, together with an example and a practice. The subjects for contemplation consist chiefly of the mysteries in which Mary figured so prominently, and the idea of which was suggested by a French book entitled *Mois de Marie.* These meditations are equally appropriate to the days set apart

---

VII. enriched this practice with such numerous indulgences, and this in virtue of a rescript of the Sacred Congregation of Indulgences, to all those who, in company with others, or alone, should, throughout the month of May, practise special devotions, or perform certain works of charity in honour of the Mother of God. The Holy Father granted 300 days' indulgence for each day throughout the month; and a general indulgence once during the month, on the usual conditions, *i.e.*, Confession, Communion, and Prayer for the Holy Father's intentions. This is in virtue of a decree of Pius IX., dated 8th August, 1859: this indulgence can also be gained on the 1st June. (See Indulgences, their origin and use, compiled by Fr. Joseph Schneider, 6th edition, Paderborn, 1878.)

in honour of the Blessed Virgin. The prayer after meditation is also an exposition of the titles holy Church applies to our Lady, in the Litany of Loretto. And, as pious narrations, the *when* and *where* of which one knows but little about, usually make but slight impression, and often are wholly disbelieved, no examples are cited in the present little work, save those extracted from the lives of eminent Saints, distinguished for their marked devotion to our Blessed Lady, and such ones as we hope may awaken a deep interest in every faithful German heart.

As regards the mode of carrying out this devotion, it suffices to follow the practice of those Churches where these devotions are publicly observed. For the rest, the following rules may prove useful:—

1. The devotions commence on the eve of May-day. A fitting place having been selected, such as a chapel or room, an image of our Lady is placed in a conspicuous place, decorated with flowers, &c. The

family assemble in this spot and begin the devotions with the Litany of the Blessed Virgin, and the prayer, "We fly to thy patronage," &c. Thus the whole month is dedicated to the most blessed Mother of God; each one places himself beneath her powerful protection, supplicating some special grace, for self or others, as the case may be. But it is well that a favour of some magnitude should be entreated for.

2. At a certain hour, daily, the points of the meditation are read aloud, slowly and distinctly, a pause sufficient for meditation being made between each point, so that the truths forming the subject of contemplation may take the deeper hold upon the mind, be applied by each to his own individual case, that thus the meditation may afford the richer fruit.

3. It is to be wished that at least half, or quarter, of an hour should be devoted to the meditation. After this is completed, one person, in the name of the united assembly, reads aloud the prayer for the day.

4. The examples may be read privately, or in common with the others. The teaching, or practice, is also to be carefully studied.

5. The Rosary may also be recited, in common, or alone. Mass should be heard daily, in Mary's honour, and a visit paid to some church or oratory dedicated to her, or a visit paid to her image. During the day the heart should be raised to Heaven in pious ejaculations.

6. Certainly you can offer our Blessed Lady no more acceptable offering, nor one that can benefit yourself more than the conquest of some sinful habit, or leading fault (striven against out of love to Jesus and His Virgin Mother), which, hitherto, has been the chief obstacle in your heavenly course. If we offer this tribute to Mary throughout the month, we shall certainly find ready access to her ear, and win great blessings in return.

7. The month should commence and terminate with Holy Communion. The devo-

tions conclude with the final meditation and the act of consecration, page xiii. This act can be made frequently during the month, but especially after receiving the Holy Eucharist. Recourse may be had to other devotional books, foremost among others, to St. Alphonsus Liguori's "Visits to the Blessed Sacrament, and to our Lady".

8. These devotions can be read at any period of the year, when Mary is to be supplicated for any special grace, such as light to discern one's vocation, &c.; and we may rest assured that this practice will be of the greatest service to us.

At the end of the Manual are appended a few short prayers for Morning and Evening; for Mass, Confession, and Holy Communion; together with some hymns in Mary's honour. And we hope and desire, in this way, to stir up the hearts of the faithful more and more, that they may glow with ever-increasing love and homage to the Mother of Mercy. Amen!

ACT OF CONSECRATION.

Most holy Virgin, and Mother of God! sinful though I am, I cast myself on my knees before thee, in presence of Almighty God and the whole host of Heaven, choosing thee to-day for my protectress, my Mother, and my Advocate with thy Divine Son, Jesus. To thee do I consecrate myself—body and soul, with all I have and am. Above all, I dedicate my heart to thee, and desire that henceforth it may be thine and thy Divine Son's alone. To thee do I consecrate the prayers and devotional practices of the present month; entreating thee to obtain for me those graces of which I stand in most urgent need, and which will be most profitable to me, to wit. . . . Show thyself my Mother; and prove that

thou forsakest none who have recourse to thee with childlike, trusting hearts. Guide my feet, that I may keep the commandments of thy Son. Stand by me in all my undertakings, and do with me as may seem best in thy sight, for I desire nought save that which is in accordance with thy will. O my gracious Mother! entreat Jesus to grant me grace to remain faithful to thee and thy Divine Son even to my latest breath. May I ever love and glorify thee in time, so that through thee, and with thee, in company with all the Angels and Saints, I may love and praise JESUS throughout all Eternity. Amen!

CONTENTS.

	PAGE
1st Day,	1
2nd Day.—The Immaculate Conception. 1st Part,	5
3rd Day.—The Immaculate Conception. 2nd Part,	11
4th Day.—The Immaculate Conception. 3rd Part,	17
5th Day.—The Nativity of Mary. 1st Part,	22
6th Day.—Nativity of the Blessed Virgin. 2nd Part,	29
7th Day.—Mary's Birth. 3rd Part,	36
8th Day.—Mary's Acts of Sacrifice. 1st Part,	40
9th Day.—Mary's Acts of Sacrifice. 2nd Part,	45
10th Day.—Mary's Sacrifice. 3rd Part,	50
11th Day.—The Annunciation. 1st Part,	56
12th Day.—The Annunciation. 2nd Part,	61
13th Day.—The Annunciation. 3rd Part,	67
14th Day.—The Visitation. 1st Part,	72
15th Day.—The Visitation. 2nd Part,	78
16th Day.—The Visitation. 3rd Part,	84
17th Day.—The Purification of the Blessed Virgin. 1st Part,	89
18th Day.—The Purification. 2nd Part,	95
19th Day.—The Purification. 3rd Part,	100
20th Day.—The Dolours of our Lady. 1st Part,	105
21st Day.—The Dolours of our Lady. 2nd Part,	110

CONTENTS.

	PAGE
22nd Day.—The Dolours of our Lady. 3rd Part,	115
23rd Day.—The Joys of Mary. 1st Part,	123
24th Day.—The Joys of Mary. 2nd Part,	129
25th Day.—The Joys of Mary. 3rd Part,	136
26th Day.—Mary's Life. 1st Part,	143
27th Day.—Mary's Life. 2nd Part,	150
28th Day.—Mary's Life. 3rd Part,	157
29th Day.—The Assumption. 1st Part,	163
30th Day.—The Assumption. 2nd Part,	170
31st Day.—3rd Part,	178
Concluding Meditation,	182
Morning Prayers,	190
Litany of Loretto,	194
Evening Prayers,	197
Devotions for Mass,	202
Devotions for Confession,	219
Devotions for Communion,	226
Aspirations after Communion,	231
Acts of Devotion, Praise, &c.,	233
Prayers to the Blessed Virgin,	237
Hymns to the Blessed Virgin,	241

Errata.

Page 65, lines 7 and 26, *for* Confraternity *read* Congregation.
„ 97, line 9, *for* Ferrar *read* Ferrer.
„ 116, „ 17, *for* HIS PHYSICAL *read* HIS MENTAL.

MONTH OF MARY.

1st DAY.

Three motives which should prompt thee to honour Mary specially throughout this month; she is thy Sovereign Mistress, thy Advocate, thy Mother.

1. MARY IS THY QUEEN AND MISTRESS; THOU, HER SERVANT. "Thou art my Sovereign Lady and Mother of my Lord!" says St. Hildephonsus. Truly—thou art the Mother of our Lord, Mother of our Creator, Mother of our Redeemer, Queen of Angels and men, and also our Queen and gracious Lady. And inasmuch as it behoves a good servant to render true and faithful service, do thou, O Christian, arouse thyself that thou mayest render zealous homage to thy Queen, and do thy utmost, especially throughout this month, to ensure her assistance and win her favour. If success crown thine efforts, truly happy wilt thou be!

2. MARY IS THY ADVOCATE; THOU, HER CLIENT. St. Ephraim thus addresses the Blessed Virgin:

"Thou art the mightiest, the sole Advocate of sinners"; and the Church designates her the Refuge of sinners, and Comforter of the afflicted. A client does all in his power to secure his patron's influence and favour. Art thou not weak and miserable in the highest degree? Dost thou not stand in need of the aid and protection of this gracious and powerful Virgin? Dost thou not need the intercession of this Mother of Mercy, to enable thee to find favour with her Son, thy Creator and thy Judge? Therefore I urge thee to render all possible homage to her throughout this month, and make it thy daily endeavour to become more worthy of her powerful intercession.

3. Mary is thy heavenly Mother; thou, her child. "She is," as St. Augustine says, "Mother of Christ's members," which members, in virtue of our Baptism, we are. What well-trained child but is anxious to seize every opportunity to testify his love and respect for his mother, in order to gladden her heart thereby?—What mother so worthy of love, so kind and gracious to us as Mary?—Dost thou desire to testify thy filial love to her? This month presents thee with an opportunity of so doing; dedicate it to her, daily practice some devotion, some good works in her honour; be faithful in observing these meditations,

lend a willing ear to thy Mother's voice, and to the holy inspirations which from time to time may fall to thy share. Then only, wilt thou deserve to be called a child of Mary, if thou keepest the commandments of her Son, and leadest a life worthy of such a Mother.

PRAYER.

Holy Mary, pray for us.

Holy Mary, with feelings of the deepest reverence and joy we utter thy name; thou art indeed our Queen, our light, and Star of the Sea. This, thy title, is as honourable to thee as it is full of consolation and delight to us. O Mary! thy blessed name illumines this dark world, shedding grace and blessing around, and filling every heart with rays of sweetest hope. He who knows and invokes thee, has no ground for doubt or fear. Make us experience the truth of this; lead us on in the way of salvation, be our beacon amid the dark surging waves of life's ocean, our protection through our pilgrimage here below, and may Thy name and that of Thy Divine Son be the last utterances of our dying lips, our final breath, our last thought, be: JESUS! MARY! Amen.

Example.

St. Matilda.

As St. Matilda was one day reading the dying Saviour's last words to His blessed Mother: "Woman, behold thy son!" she felt herself constrained to entreat our Divine Lord to grant her the same grace which He had bestowed on St. John, and that He would say of her to His Mother, "Woman, behold thy daughter!" Scarcely had she framed her petition, than her wish was granted. She distinctly saw Jesus commending her to His Mother's care, enjoining upon her that she should, in virtue of His Cross and Passion and of the special love He bore Matilda, take the Saint under her maternal protection. Rejoiced at this, St. Matilda ventured to add one more request: that this favour should be extended to all who should make the like supplication, and our Lord replied that no earnest, zealous suppliant should be refused. —This should indeed encourage us to approach Him with the like petition. Let us choose Mary for our Mother, and so act that we may be worthy of this great Saviour.

Practice.

As soon as you awake, offer all your actions to Jesus and to Mary.

2ND DAY.

On the Immaculate Conception.

1ST PART.

Mary was conceived without sin, because she is the daughter of the Eternal Father, and this by creation, adoption and redemption.

1. MARY IS THE DAUGHTER OF THE ETERNAL FATHER, AND THIS IN VIRTUE OF CREATION. To her the Church applies those words: "As the first born of all creatures, I proceeded from the mouth of the Eternal."—Therefore must Mary be distinguished from, and take precedence of, all other creatures. From all eternity had she been predestined to be Mother of the Eternal Son, consequently it behoved that the Mother of such a Son should be free from all stain of sin, and thus was it with her from the very moment of her conception. But how is it with me? What is my leading characteristic? In what does my conduct differ from that of the majority of sinners and unbelievers? Does my daily life testify to my being a child of God?

Alas! the contrary may be the case! if so, what a contrast to Mary! What woe for me!

2. MARY IS THE DAUGHTER OF THE ETERNAL FATHER, AND THIS IN VIRTUE OF HER ADOPTION. As such, she was endowed with the prerogatives and graces befitting the daughter of such a Father. In her the Eternal manifested the riches of His love, lavishing on her the graces requisite to render her well-pleasing in His sight. THOU ART FULL OF GRACE! Therefore it behoved her to be free from all sin, spotless and undefiled, holy as is the Eternal Father.—Thou too, although by nature a child of wrath, art by Baptism a child of God. What value dost thou attach to this inestimable privilege? Alas! how often hast thou not disgraced thy lofty birth! This thought should fill thee with shame and confusion!

3. MARY IS THE DAUGHTER OF THE ETERNAL FATHER, BOTH BY GRACE AND BY REDEMPTION. If Mary's redemption, that is, her preservation from original sin, is due to the merits of her Divine Son, the Eternal Father shares therein inasmuch as her freedom from sin was the work of the Blessed Trinity. Therefore it was that God told the serpent that a woman should crush his head, and wholly subdue and conquer him.—Dost thou, by thy courageous resistance of temptation, crush the

serpent's head, or hast thou cowardly yielded to temptation? Conscience will provide thee with a reply. If thou art guilty in this respect, lament thy sin, and amend thy ways. Mary is waiting to aid thee with her potent intercession.

PRAYER.

Holy Mother of God, pray for us.

Holy Mother of God, as far as a mere creature can do so, thou hast merited this glorious name, for truly thou art the Mother of the Incarnate God, and thy sanctity and thy virtues have entitled thee to bear this lofty appellation. Mother, far exalted above all creatures, thou wert chosen out from the daughters of Zion to be the mother of the Divine Son. Blessed art thou among women, and blessed is the fruit of thy womb, JESUS CHRIST, very God and very man. With deep humility and admiring faith do we exclaim: *Pray for us, O Holy Mother of God!* Thou art the mother of Him who is our Redeemer and our God: but thou art also the Mother of sinners, for whom Thy Divine Son shed His Blood. Intercede for us with JESUS that we may participate in His merits, and beg for us grace to love Him with all our heart and all our strength. Amen.

EXAMPLE.

The Council of Ephesus.

In the fifth century Nestorius was Bishop of Constantinople. He was a man full of pride and haughtiness, who sought to conceal an ungodly heart beneath the guise of outward piety, until at last his arrogance assumed such a degree that he attempted to rob the humblest of the children of men of her most sublime title, and then dared to preach that it was not allowable to assign to Mary the title of *Mother of God*. Such teaching awoke the greatest displeasure among his hearers. The whole of the city was roused, and every heart was both grieved and indignant at the insults offered to the Divine Mother. Saintly and hoary hermits left their cells in order to take their part in the public assemblies to defend the cause of their Celestial Queen, and guard the faithful from the false teaching of Nestorius. The bishops and pastors of the Church, well knowing that if the Blessed Virgin were robbed of this title the whole mystery of the Redemption would fall to the ground, strove zealously in defence of this dogma.

A Council was called at Ephesus, to which the

bishops flocked from all sides, in which council (in the name of Pope Celestine) pre-eminence was assigned to St. Cyril, Patriarch of Alexandria. The godless Nestorius, refusing to abjure his error, was judged and condemned as a heretic. It is impossible to describe the universal joy with which Christendom hailed this decision, so glorious for Mary. On the day when the Church was to publish her decision regarding Mary's lofty prerogative, nearly the whole city was congregated together outside the Church where the bishops were assembled. They remained there all day long, as if nought were so dear to them as Mary's honour. At last, the doors were thrown open, St. Cyril appeared at the head of more than 200 bishops and announced to the people the Church's condemnation of Nestorius and his accursed doctrine. Hardly was the sentence pronounced, than shouts of joy rent the air, the whole city resounded with hymns in Mary's praise, and the universal and joyous cry of the faithful was: The Virgin's foe is vanquished. Long live Mary! the great, the sublime, the glorious Mother of God! Long live Mary!—The Fathers of the Council were escorted home by torch-light, amid the applause and blessings of the people, and the streets through which they passed were redolent

with costly incense. The whole city was magnificently illuminated, and everything done to celebrate the day on which Mary won such a glorious victory over her foe.

PRACTICE.

When you awake in the morning, promise the exalted Mother of God that you would rather die than voluntarily offend Jesus by one act of mortal sin.

3rd Day.

The Immaculate Conception.

2nd Part.

Mary was conceived without sin: it behoved that she who was exalted to such a lofty dignity as to be the chosen mother of the Eternal Word, and who was to be so full of merit, should know no spot of sin.

1. THE HONOUR CONFERRED ON MARY. She was chosen to be the Mother of the second Person in the Blessed Trinity; a rank more exalted than any save that of the three Divine Persons. Therefore it behoved that she should possess a purity second only to that of God Himself, that she should be free from original sin.—Ah! how pure and lovely is thy heavenly Mother! how impure and sullied art thou, in comparison with her!

2. MARY'S MERITS. These were to far exceed those of any other Saint, inasmuch as Mary would faithfully correspond with the grace vouchsafed her from the very beginning. MANY DAUGHTERS HAVE DONE WELL; BUT THOU EXCEEDEST THEM ALL. A few Saints, such as St. John Baptist and the Prophet Jeremiah, were sanctified in their mother's

womb; but Mary, the Mother of the Redeemer and the Queen of Saints, was immaculate from her conception, and such it behoved her to be who was to take precedence of all other creatures.— Pause, admire the inestimable privilege conferred on the Blessed Virgin, and ask thyself what use thou hast made of the many spiritual graces God has conferred on thee, whether thou hast laid up treasure for Heaven or Hell?

3. THE HONOUR RESERVED FOR MARY. As mother of her Divine Son, Mary was to rank above the Celestial Choirs and reign as Queen of Heaven and Earth. Nothing is so dear to a good son as the honour of his mother. How then could He Who is incarnate purity and sanctity, have permitted His Mother to have remained one sole instant in Satan's power? The mere thought of such a possibility fills us with shuddering alarm!

Reflect then, O my soul, how displeasing it must be to God to see Satan triumph at thy voluntary subjection to his sway.

PRAYER.

Holy Virgin of Virgins, pray for us!

O holiest and purest of Virgins, well dost thou

merit this title, thou who wast a Virgin although a Mother. This thy purity won thee the heart of God; by thy example, thou hast drawn all Virgins to follow in thy train, and succourest them with thine efficient aid.

Virgin of Virgins, pray for us! Help us to tread in thy footsteps, to mortify all carnal desires, so that we may guard the precious gem of purity, unsullied.

EXAMPLE.

St. Alphonsus Rodriguez.

The wise man's words: *I love them that love me,* are put by the Church on Mary's lips, and rightly so, for never has any one trusted in her, or given her his affection, without being the recipient of the most touching proofs of her love and tender care.

St. Alphonsus Rodriguez is a striking example of the truth of this assertion. He was a lay-brother of the Society of Jesus, and seemed with his mother's milk to have imbibed his love for Mary. As a child, his love for her was remarkable, he would seek out her images, press them to his heart, kiss them with deep affection, and address the most fervent prayers to her whose likeness they bore. When hardly five years old, he thus

addressed her in the fulness of his infantine love: "Didst thou but know the depth of my affection for thee! My love for thee is more than thine for me." Hardly had he uttered these words, than Mary appeared to him, saying: "What is this thou sayest, my son? Know that my love for thee is so great that thine can never equal it."

As he grew up, his love for Mary went on increasing, so that he might with truth be termed Mary's servant, so wholly did he consecrate himself to her service and that of her Divine Son.

In his later years, when porter in the College at Majorca, the rosary was constantly in his hand, and after his death it was discovered that the skin of his thumb and forefinger was perfectly hard from so constantly telling his beads. But the Immaculate Conception was the chief object of his devotion.

His whole countenance and words glowed with ardent love whenever this mystery was alluded to. He urged everyone to practice this devotion, specially recommending it to young people as the most powerful aid in obtaining purity of heart. In all his trials he fled to Mary, and was succoured. One day he was a prey to the most distressing doubts. He at once had recourse to his wonted weapon, and began to recite the

rosary. In order to add to the efficacy of his prayer, he added to the words, Hail Mary! full of grace, these: "*Holy Mary, Mother of God, remember me*". But as the temptation, instead of vanishing, grew but the stronger, he prayed the more fervently, and with a louder voice: "Be mindful of me, O Mother, come to my aid, for I perish!" Then the Celestial Helper appeared to him, dissipated his temptations, and filled his soul with sweetest consolation.

The same fervour was frequently vouchsafed him through life, and in a special manner on his death-bed, when the wicked foe having besieged him with varying temptations, at last plunged him in a state of great despondency, almost bordering on despair. Alphonsus bore all this with patience and resignation to the Divine Will, placing his trust in God and Mary, incessantly invoking the Blessed Virgin to come to his relief: his prayer was at last granted. Jesus and Mary appeared to him, encouraging him to endure patiently the remaining few moments of suffering he was destined to undergo, for his death was to be a painful one. And so it was indeed; but hardly had he invoked Jesus and Mary in the moment of his severe suffering, than he received aid and strength to bear his pains with patience and with joy.

How efficacious is *true devotion* to Mary, and how many are the graces we receive when we invoke her in the name of her Immaculate Conception! Let us often draw nigh to her with the following words on our lips, words that have proved efficacious to many a Christain. Morning and evening let us address her thus:

BY THY IMMACULATE CONCEPTION AND SPOTLESS VIRGINITY, DO THOU, O MOST PURE VIRGIN, PURIFY MY HEART, MY BODY, AND MY SOUL, IN THE NAME OF THE FATHER, ✣ OF THE SON ✣ AND OF THE HOLY GHOST. ✣ Amen.

PRACTICE.

Be very careful to make your daily meditation in a befitting manner.

4th Day.

The Immaculate Conception.

3rd Part.

Mary was conceived without sin, that she might be worthy of her Divine Spouse and be a fitting recipient of His Grace.

1. THE GIFTS OF THE HOLY GHOST. A bridegroom can refuse nothing to his beloved. What could Mary desire more earnestly than to be all-pure and beautiful in the eyes of her heavenly Spouse? Could the Holy Ghost refuse to grant the request of one so dear to Himself? Why is thy soul so rarely bedewed by celestial graces? Surely it is because of thine indifference.

2. THE HOLY GHOST'S GENEROSITY TO MARY. Recall the Holy Ghost's goodness to St. John Baptist and to Jeremiah, who, through His mercy, were sanctified by Him in their mother's womb, then reflect how far more abundant must have been the grace bestowed by Him on Mary. So greatly was she favoured that she was preserved from all stain of sin, and endowed with every

grace and blessing. Congratulate Mary on her freedom from sin, and think of the debt of gratitude you owe that same Spirit for the many graces He has conferred on you.

3. THE HOLY GHOST ENRICHED MARY. Holiness being the distinguishing characteristic of all pertaining to God, and Mary's conception being so intimately associated with that of Jesus, the Holy of Holies, who was conceived by the Holy Ghost, it behoved her to be conceived without sin in order that she might share the purity of her Divine Spouse. Therefore sin never had dominion over her, her sanctity was unsullied and her purity such as befitted the Spouse of the Holy Ghost. *Thy* life should be one of consecration to God,— is it holy and worthy of Him?

PRAYER.

Mother of Christ, pray for us.

Mother of Christ, thou art that holy and happy Mother of the Incarnate God who so loved us that He deigned to associate our humanity to His Divinity; hence, He has become our Head, and has made us His own members in Holy Baptism. As we are one with Jesus, thou, Mother of our Head, art our Mother too; therefore take pity

on us thy children, intercede for us with JESUS, thy Son, our Head, that He may have mercy on us, and grant us grace to walk worthy of our vocation, that we may be His through time and throughout eternity. Amen.

EXAMPLE.

St. Francis Xavier.

The great Apostle of India, St. Francis Xavier, had, throughout his whole life, a marked devotion to the Mother of God, for whom he entertained the deepest reverence and affection. On the Feast of the Assumption, in company with St. Ignatius and his companions, he repaired to the Church at Montmartre (hill of Martyrs; dedicated to the Blessed Virgin), and there vowed themselves to the service of God. It was in the Church of Loretto that he was first inspired with the desire of evangelising India. He never commenced any undertaking without placing it under the Blessed Virgin's protection. When teaching or preaching, he addressed himself to Mary for aid and light, concluding his instructions with the words: "Hail to thee, O Queen". In the many difficulties he encountered during his Apostolate, he placed himself ever under her mighty protec-

tion, and to her he attributed his escape from the numerous dangers which surrounded him. As a badge of his devotion to Mary, he usually wore a rosary round his neck, and in order to inspire the newly-converted with faith in the efficacy of the prayers addressed to her, he wrought many wonderful miracles by its aid. A merchant of Meliapur, about to sail for Malacca, asked the Saint for some parting souvenir. St. Francis gave him his own rosary, saying: "This will be of great service to you, if only you have confidence in Mary". Hardly had they weighed anchor, when a fearful storm arose which dashed the ship to pieces on a neighbouring rock. There appeared no chance of safety for the crew, when the merchant, remembering St. Francis Xavier's parting injunction, and trusting confidently in Mary's help, grasped his rosary in his hand, and instantly the whole party found themselves, how, they knew not, safe on shore.

The Apostle of India and Japan had a special devotion to the Immaculate Conception, which he had vowed to uphold and defend. He often had recourse to Mary for the conversion of great sinners, as also to obtain forgiveness for his own transgressions. He says in one of his letters: " I have taken the Queen of Heaven as my Patroness

that so I may obtain pardon for my innumerable sins". In his preaching, he frequently made Mary's lofty qualities his theme in order to encourage his hearers to honour and love this Mother of Mercy. And in his last moments, far from all human consolation, Mary was his hope, his refuge, and support; and his dying prayer, uttered with child-like devotion and indescribable delight, was this: " Monstrate esse matrem."— " Show thyself my Mother!"

PRACTICE.

Hear Mass with the greatest reverence and devotion.

5TH DAY.

THE NATIVITY OF MARY.

1ST PART.

At Mary's birth, Heaven rejoiced because she would repair its loss, increase its glory, and reign as its Queen.

1. MARY WAS SENT INTO THE WORLD IN ORDER TO REPAIR THE LOSS SUSTAINED BY HEAVEN. To her, Heaven is indebted for the countless numbers of the elect redeemed by the Blood of her Divine Son. How must not Heaven have rejoiced at the birth of such a Mother! O that Angels and Saints may one day rejoice at my bliss! But that depends entirely on myself. God's grace will not fail me, if I but respond thereto. Am I really in earnest about my salvation?

2. BY MARY'S BIRTH, HEAVEN'S GLORY IS AUGMENTED. A God-Incarnate, a Virgin-Mother, a countless host of ransomed souls, must of necessity increase, in no slight degree, the radiance of the celestial glory. Good ground, indeed, had Heaven to rejoice at Mary's birth because of the honour

which would accrue to it therefrom. Pause, O Christian, and see whether thy actions are a source of joy to Heaven or to Hell. Think of Mary, invoke her, and follow her example!

3. MARY WAS DESTINED TO BE QUEEN OF HEAVEN. In virtue of having been elected from all eternity to be Mother of the Eternal Word, and because of the exalted rank to which her virtues and her sanctity would entitle her, Mary was a Queen from the first moment of her birth. A nation's joy at the birth of an heir to the throne may give you some faint idea of the joy the Angels experienced at Mary's nativity. Strive to win her favour now, that you may hereafter love and praise her as your Queen throughout eternity. Amen.

PRAYER.

Mother of Divine Grace, pray for us.

O blessed, happy Mother of Jesus, the Author and Giver of all grace, full of grace art thou. From the first moment of thy conception God preserved thee from all stain of sin. By thy holy, perfect life, thou hast augmented the graces wherewith thy Creator had endowed thee. Thou art the Channel by which Heaven's graces flow

down to us. Look graciously on thy children, behold how we, by our sins, have forfeited all claim to grace. Compassionate our misery, aid us from the abundance of thy fulness, and entreat thy Son JESUS that He would grant us grace that we may be well-pleasing in His sight and thine, and remain faithful unto death. Amen.

EXAMPLE.

Pope Pius V.—The victory of Lepanto, and the defeat of the Turks before Vienna.

The famous victory of Lepanto (in the Ionian Archipelago), in which the Turks were wholly defeated, will be a lasting memorial of Mary's special protection. For more than a century the Turks had filled the whole of Christendom with terror and dismay. They gained victory after victory, and this was permitted by God for the chastisement and humiliation of His erring children, that He might thereby awake their faith, and manifest His own power and might, as well as Mary's glory, by the wonders He was about to effect. The Sultan, Selim (son of Soliman, and his successor on the throne), having taken Cypress from the Venetians, was puffed up by his success,

and meditated nothing less than subjugating the whole of Christendom to his sway.

At this time, Pius V. was sitting in Peter's Chair, a man full of zeal and faith, a faithful adherent of Mary, in the efficacy of whose intercession he had the greatest reliance. This Pope (afterwards canonized, whose Feast the Church celebrates on May 5), was overwhelmed with dismay at the threatened danger. But, full of confidence in the Blessed Virgin, he formed an alliance with the Venetians and the Spaniards to repel their common foe. As the two fleets were separated and all inter-communication impossible, there seemed, humanly speaking, no chance of overcoming the overwhelming numbers of their adversaries; but the Holy Father's trust failed not for a single instant, so convinced was he of the Blessed Virgin's help, to obtain which he set apart a day of fasting and humiliation, urging the whole body of the faithful to call upon Mary for aid. Nearly the whole of Europe was on its knees; processions and other devotions were organized in Mary's honour; and on bestowing his benediction to Don John of Austria (the Commander of the Christian fleet) the Holy Father assured him of victory. At the same time he gave orders that all soldiers who were

only intent on plunder, or led a godless life, should be dismissed, in order not to draw down the Divine malediction on the whole army. Like Moses, Pius raised his hands to Heaven in constant prayer, invoking Mary, the Mother of Mercy, to obtain victory for the Christians. On the 7th October, 1571, the battle of Lepanto was fought. Both sides fought with unflinching courage, and, for a moment, victory seemed to be on the side of the Turks. But Mary heard the petitions of the faithful. The God of Armies gave the victory into the hands of the Christians. The Turks were totally defeated, they lost more than 30,000 men, and their terror-inspiring fleet was for ever robbed of its power. At the very moment the victory was won, the Holy Father was cognisant of the fact. He was discussing business matters with the Cardinals, when suddenly he became silent, and after raising his eyes heavenwards for a few moments, exclaimed: "Away now with all business; it behoves us to do no less than return thanks to God for the victory He has given us". The result proved that at the very moment he uttered these words, the Christians had won the day. And the Holy Pontiff, who had been supernaturally made acquainted with the result of the contest, was so

fully convinced that the victory was due to Mary's protection, that, for a perpetual remembrance of the same, he caused these words to be inserted in the Litany of Loretto : HELP OF CHRISTIANS, PRAY FOR US. He also instituted a special Feast Day, which, during the Pontificate of Pope Gregory XIII., was fixed to take place on the first Sunday of October, under the title of THE FEAST OF THE ROSARY. By the Blessed Virgin's assistance, a similar victory was gained over the Turks, in Vienna, in the year 1683, during the reign of Leopold I. The Turks surrounded the city with 316,000 men, and many instruments of war. The whole land had been laid desolate; thousands of Christians had been put to death in the most cruel manner, or made slaves, and even greater misfortune seemed imminent, but throughout every province Mary's name was invoked, and public processions and pilgrimages made in her honour. When the danger seemed at the climax, Mary came to the relief of the faithful. On the 12th September, the Turks, far outnumbering their adversaries, were attacked and wholly routed by the Christians. As an eternal memento of gratitude for this favour, Pope Innocent XI. ordained that the first Sunday after the Feast of the Nativity of the Blessed Virgin should be

universally and perpetually observed as the Feast of the Holy Name of Mary. How then does it not behove us to have recourse, in all our dangers and necessities, to her whom the Church herself has named the " Help of Christians ".

PRACTICE.

Pray daily for the blessing of a good death.

6TH DAY.

NATIVITY OF THE BLESSED VIRGIN.

2ND PART.

Earth rejoiced at Mary's birth, because she was to be the Mother of our Redeemer, and our Advocate, and Mother.

1. **MARY IS THE MOTHER OF OUR REDEEMER.** How great is Mary's love for the human race! Nothing is dearer to her than our redemption and salvation. She who was destined to give birth to the Redeemer of mankind, was also to play an important part in the great work of the atonement. Yes, she was to offer up her Divine Son for our redemption and win us eternal bliss. Well may earth rejoice at Mary's birth! Her appearance was the blessed dawn announcing the rising of the Sun of Righteousness. Rejoice, O ye lovers of Jesus, ye who look to Him for salvation! Weep and lament, all ye that love the works of sin and darkness! Yes, bewail your misery! for you, Mary was bereft of her Son, and you scorn her gifts!

2. MARY IS THE ADVOCATE OF THE HUMAN RACE. As mother of our Redeemer, Mary regards us as her own possession. She knows how costly was the ransom paid for us, therefore she never ceases to intercede that none may be eternally lost. She compassionates our needs, and incessantly supplicates the Divine Judge on our behalf. O happy world, to possess so potent an Advocate! Ah! had not Mary extended her maternal protection to thee, turning aside the punishment due to thy sins, what would have been thy fate? Remember that she has exerted herself on thy behalf, in order that thou mayest amend and reform thy life.

3. MARY IS OUR GOOD MOTHER. As Eve is the mother of us all, in Jesus, Mary is our Mother; she has given us new life, a life of grace and eternal salvation. In Eve we die, through Mary we have eternal life and a blessed immortality. In order that we might rightly understand this truth, our Crucified Redeemer bequeathed us to His blessed Mother, as her children, desiring that from thenceforth she should regard and treat us as such. Had not earth then good cause for joy, when Mary came into the world? Does my life and conduct harmonize with the relationship I bear to so pure a Mother?

Prayer.

Mother most pure, Mother most chaste; Mother inviolate, Mother undefiled, pray for us.

O Mother, so chaste, so pure, so undefiled! Words fail to express thy incomparable and ever unsullied purity. Thou art the Mother of our Lord and Redeemer, and this, without detriment to thy virginity. O Virgin-Mother! by thy immaculate purity, defend us from every foe that would fain rob us of that priceless gem. Mother most pure, make us pure, that we may be pleasing in thine eyes. Amen.

Example.

St. Dominic.

St. Dominic was born in Old Castile, in the year 1170, and was chosen by Providence as an elect vessel whose mission it was to shed abroad the light of the gospel, and refute the heresy of the Albegensians, who then sorely vexed the Church and wrought sad havoc in France. This renowned servant of God was unwearied in preaching the gospel; and his holy life, and the numerous miracles God worked by his instrumentality, testified to the

truth of his doctrine. Devotion to Mary was, so he assures us, the chief weapon with which he waged war against the heretics. Never did he commence any sermon, or instruction, without first kneeling down and entreating Mary's aid in the following words: "Grant, O holy Virgin, that I may proclaim thy praise, and strengthen me to withstand thy foes". His efforts were not in vain. Many heretics were converted. But the results fell short of the saintly man's expectations; many remained plunged in heresy, and closed their ears to the voice of truth. St. Dominic made this a matter of lamentation to the Blessed Virgin, and Mary, in the year 1206, exhorted him to have recourse to the Angelic Salutation (that Salutation whereby God paved the way for the annunciation of the sublime mystery of the Incarnation), and to teach the people the use of the Rosary, that he might at once experience the blessed fruits that would ensue from the practice of this devotion. Dominic followed the advice of the holy Mother of God; and his confidence in her was abundantly rewarded. In lieu of controversy, he set to work expounding to the people the Rosary, its use, and mysteries. In this way he won more souls than by all his previous efforts; his preaching was marked by increased

vigour and unction, melting the hardest hearts, and leading countless wanderers back to the Church's fold—Therefore is the use of the Rosary so strictly enjoined upon us, and, to encourage us in this practice, the Church has promised numerous indulgences and graces to such as recite the Rosary in a spirit of devotion, and full confidence in Mary. If in earnest as regards our own and our neighbour's salvation, let us have recourse to the Rosary, always reciting it with attention, and meditating upon each mystery of our salvation; in a word, reciting it in the spirit of the Church, then will the practice of this devotion win for us innumerable graces. Before all our undertakings, let us say at least one " Hail Mary," that under her mighty protection, success may crown our efforts.

PRACTICE.

Frequently make a Spiritual Communion, i.e., awake within your heart the most fervent desire to receive your Divine Lord, by a worthy Communion, that you may be united eternally to Him.

7TH DAY.

MARY'S BIRTH.

3RD PART.

Hell lamented at Mary's birth, because she was destined to be its vanquisher.

1. MARY WAS BORN THAT SHE MIGHT WAGE WAR AGAINST THE POWERS OF HELL. In Eden, God declared to the serpent that there should be continued emnity between him and the Blessed Virgin! the consequences of this emnity have ever since been experienced by Hell. In Mary, they become strong and victorious, whom Satan viewed as puny and weak. What profound grief, what a sense of endless loss the infernal spirits must have felt when she appeared on earth, who was to be their vigorous opponent, their mighty Victor!

How is it with thee, O reader! Art thou a source of joy, or lamentation, to Satan and his hellish crew?

2. MARY WAS BORN TO CONQUER HELL. With Mary, warfare is synonymous with victory: you

will be convinced of this if you remember how the infernal spirits have ever trembled at Mary's name; how, at its sound, those possessed of devils have been cured, and many a sinner converted by Mary's intercession. Note this, O Christian soul; Mary will arm thee for the fight, and aid thee to surmount the dangers which surround thy soul. Flee to Mary for succour, invoke her name, place thyself beneath her maternal protection, trust in her assistance, which will never, never, fail thee.

3. Mary was born that the powers of Hell might be disarmed. It was not enough for Mary that she should conquer Satan; she must disarm and rob him of his power. Therefore she crushes his head beneath her feet, to show that he is utterly defeated, and that he is henceforth powerless to injure us, if we are on our guard. Dost thou oft-times complain of his craft, and power, and thy own weakness to resist him? Wouldst thou be screened from his attacks? Flee with steadfast trust to Mary; she will intercede for thee with her Son, and win thee strength and vigour, not only to resist Satan's temptations, but to gain a complete victory over him, and even to turn his temptations to good account. Never has it been known that any one who had recourse to Mary was left unaided.

Prayer.

Mother most amiable, Mother most admirable, pray for us.

O Mother, most amiable and admirable! By the plenitude of thy perfection thou didst ravish the heart of the Celestial King: as the Virgin-Mother, thou art the wonder and admiration of Angels and of men. O wondrous Mother, thou art all lovely and glorious! Virgin and Mother too! loftiest, yet lowliest of all created beings, thou esteemest thyself as nought, yet in thy Creator's sight, thou art the most blessed and most perfect of all. Kind and gracious Mother, pray for us; win us grace to love thee with a most tender love, that we may thereby grow in love to Jesus, Thy Son. Amen.

Example.

St. Elizabeth.

St. Elizabeth, daughter of the King of Hungary, and wife of the Landgrave of Thuringia, was born in Presburg, in the year 1207. She seemed appointed by Providence to irradiate the Church in Germany during the thirteenth century, and to magnify the beauty of virtue and holiness. She was distinguished for her great and noble qualities,

and for her ardent love to our Lady. When a child, she placed herself beneath Mary's mighty protection, and chose her as her Patroness. She used every means to encourage her play-fellows to practise devotion to the Blessed Virgin, and even in the midst of her amusements would find time to raise her heart to God, and recite a Hail Mary. She retained the warmest love for Mary, endeavouring to imitate her virtues by her own purity of heart, holy simplicity, and varied works of mercy. Of all the Apostles, St. John was her favourite, inasmuch as he was the one to whose care Jesus entrusted His Blessed Mother. Although St. Elizabeth had received many favours from Mary throughout the whole course of her life, never did she receive such signal marks of her maternal protection as during the time succeeding her pious husband's death, when her brother-in-law treated her with such unkindness that he thrust her and her children out into the world, exposing them to the greatest misery. Though forsaken by man, Elizabeth experienced the truth of those words, that God forsakes none who hope in Him, and that never does any one flee for succour to her whom the Church so truly styles, "Comforter of the afflicted," and "Help of Christians," without obtaining relief.

Our Divine Lord appeared several times to St. Elizabeth, in order to comfort and strengthen her, specially commending her to His Blessed Mother's care. Mary was the channel and dispenser of all the graces and blessings she received in such rich abundance from the Lord. "If thou art willing to be my pupil, I will be thy teacher: art thou willing to be my handmaid, I will be thy mistress." Elizabeth now entrusted herself wholly to Mary's care and guidance; and this tender mother instructed her in all the sublime mysteries of God, leading her on in the path of holiness, from virtue to virtue, until she attained the highest degree of perfection, endowing her with strength to persevere in the practice of every virtue, and stedfastly pursue the thorny road of the Cross. How great was Elizabeth's progress in holiness under such a teacher! How numerous the graces bestowed by such a tender Mother! With rapid steps she drew near the goal; and ere she had completed her 24th year, God called her to Himself. Her dying words were these: " O MARY, COME TO MINE AID!" whereupon that Mother of Mercy, who had been her protector and guide in the paths of holiness, now translated her to heavenly bliss. Let us strive to emulate St. Elizabeth's love to the Blessed Virgin, by purity of heart, and deeds of

mercy to the sick and poor, whom Jesus terms His brethren, and who, as such, are so dear to His Blessed Mother. Also, let us entreat Mary to instruct us in the way of perfection, to lead and strength us, until we attain our being's end and aim, Eternal Life!

Practice.

Be kind to the poor, aiding them to the extent of your power. All that you do to them out of love to Jesus, you do to Jesus Himself.

8th Day.

Mary's Acts of Sacrifice.

1st Part.

In entering on her Hidden Life in the Temple, Mary manifested heroic virtue. 1. In renouncing home and parents at such a tender age. 2. By the motives which animated her.

1. WHAT MARY GAVE UP ? As a most perfect daughter, Mary loved her parents, Joachim and Anna, with the tenderest affection, but as soon as she heard the Divine call she forsook all in order to consecrate herself wholly to God's service. What an heroic resolve !—Does not this example fill thee with confusion ? How often hast thou shrunk from renouncing the ties that bind thee, turning a deaf ear to the voice of conscience and of God !

2. THE AGE AT WHICH MARY FORSOOK HER PARENTS. The Blessed Virgin had scarcely attained her 4th year when she dedicated herself to God in the Temple, a circumstance making her heroic virtue stand out in deeper relief. We all

know how painful it is to part from parents at such a tender age. But Mary surmounted this feeling. Therefore thy own natural inclinations and disposition will not avail thee as an excuse for disregarding the Divine Call. Rouse thy courage, cast sentiment to the winds, conquer thy own inclinations. God will aid thee in the struggle and rich will be thy reward!

3. THE MOTIVES THAT LED MARY TO QUIT HER PARENTS. Her heart was inflamed by such deep love for God, that she joyfully forsook all, that she might freely give herself wholly to her Creator. It was God's Will that she should serve Him in retirement from the world; henceforth, to her the world was nought, God was her all in all! What a striking example of Virtue!—Ah, would that my mind and heart were more deaf to the syren voices of earth! Would that I, too, could speed more rapidly onwards in the heavenly road. How many a grace would God then lavish on me.

PRAYER.

Mother of our Creator, Mother of our Saviour, pray for us.

Mother of the Almighty God, Creator of Heaven and Earth, who from all Eternity pre-

ordained thee to be His Mother! Mother of the all-merciful God, who deigned to shed the last drop of His most precious Blood for us, that He might ransom us from eternal death, and beget us to immortal life! Sublime Mother! since God chose to make thee play so predominant a part in the work of our Redemption, entreat Him to make us rich partakers of the glorious fruits of His Redemption, and vouchsafe us a new heart, wholly glowing with love to our Creator, and with love to our Divine Redeemer. Amen.

Example.

St. Casimir.

Love and devotion to the Virgin of Virgins is the characteristic trait of pure, chaste souls; no true Christian heart, that glows not with love to Mary. St. Casimir is a striking proof of this. This prince, son of Casimir III., King of Poland, from his earliest years evinced great zeal in the service of God. Jesus Crucified, and Mary the Virgin-Mother, were the chief objects of his love. He had an intense horror of luxury and sensuality, two vices unfortunately so often found in the dwellings of the rich and great. Nothing was so sacred and dear to him as innocence and purity of

heart. In order to guard these, his favourite virtues, unsullied, he placed himself beneath our Lady's special protection. And from love to her, and an earnest desire to imitate and to please her, he took the vow of chastity, and so conscientiously and faithfully did he observe it that his purity remained unsullied. Such an example must needs have been most potent, and so dear was this virtue in his eyes, that he chose rather to die than comply with his physician's counsels to prolong his life by entering the marriage-state. We have a touching proof of his tender love for Mary in the Latin hymn that bears his name. *Omni die dic Mariae mea laudes anima* (Daily, daily, sing to Mary). These words were frequently on the Saint's lips, and after making them the vehicle for the expression of his love to the Blessed Virgin throughout his life, he desired a copy of this verse to be laid in his coffin, and buried with him.

His heart was Mary's, his life was spent in praising her. He was buried in the Chapel of the Mother of God, for whom he had evinced so tender an affection, and who had so constantly watched over him with maternal love, and freed him from so many dangers. He died in the 25th year of his age, and was honoured as the tutelar Saint of Poland, the special patron of youth, and

protector of all such, who like him, strive to please Jesus and Mary by purity of heart.

Practice.

Pay a visit to the Blessed Sacrament, and also to our Lady, in some Church dedicated to her, or before one of her images.

9TH DAY.

MARY'S ACTS OF SACRIFICE.

2ND PART.

At her dedication in the Temple, Mary manifested heroic virtue; this was visible in the generosity, joy, and zeal with which she consecrated herself to God.

1. MARY'S GENEROSITY. She was not content with giving up parents, home, and possessions for God; she desired to do more, to dedicate herself wholly, body, soul, and spirit, to His service.— Compare thy conduct with hers; note how anxious thou art to make certain compromises and reservations; expressing thyself willing to lead a devout life if it involve no renunciation of friends and worldly pleasures. Dost thou not blush at thy want of resolution and moral courage?

2. THE JOY WITH WHICH MARY DEDICATED HERSELF TO GOD. Mark the cheerfulness and alacrity with which the holy child ascends the steps leading to the Temple! All eyes are fixed on her. Behold true heroism! Contrast her spirit with

thine; dost thou serve thy God with that gladness of heart, and devotion, so pleasing in the Divine sight?

3. MARY'S ZEAL. Generally speaking, the ardour of our zeal depends on the depth of our gratitude. Who so abundantly favoured as Mary? Who so grateful as she for the lofty graces, the full value of which she so well knew, and so justly appreciated. How deep and tender must have been the love which filled her heart as she dedicated herself to God within the sacred walls of the Temple!— Emulate her zeal, that thy acts of sacrifice, good deeds, and conquests over self, may be well-pleasing to the Almighty.

PRAYER.

Virgin most prudent, pray for us.

Most prudent and wise Virgin, who in all thy actions and undertakings sought but God alone, thou, whose lamp was constantly filled with the oil of good works, wherewith thou wast ever ready to meet the Heavenly Spouse, win us grace to avoid the folly and misery of the foolish virgins, that, imitating thy example, we may, by the constant practise of good works, be ready to welcome the Bridegroom of our souls. Amen.

EXAMPLE.

St. Teresa.

The Lord is ever watchful over His Church. When she is beset by foes, He manifests by the clearest tokens that He, the Omnipotent One, is her ruler and her defender. She is His beloved Bride; her honour is dear to Him; *even the gates of Hell shall not prevail against her.* Christ's promise, and the experience of 1800 years, are guarantees of this consoling truth, of which the history of the Church in the sixteenth century is a striking proof. Whilst the so-called Reformers seduced many by their false doctrines, and by their lies, calumnies, and misrepresentations endeavoured to cast disgrace on the Church and all that religion holds most dear, God raised up a multitude of holy men and women who, by their striking virtues and holy zeal more than counterbalanced the loss the Church had sustained at the hands of her foes. In the foremost rank of these saintly ones, who were living examples of Catholic doctrine and whose light was to irradiate all future ages, St. Teresa occupied the first place. Among the many virtues for which she was distinguished, devotion to Mary stood out in high relief. She

had received a Christian training at her mother's hands, and was about six years old when this devotion to the Blessed Virgin began to take still deeper root within her heart. On losing her mother in the 12th year of her age, she threw herself on her knees before our Lady's image, dedicated herself wholly to her service, begging the Blessed Virgin to be henceforth her Mother. From that moment she viewed herself as Mary's child. Later on, she joined the Carmelite Order (founded specially in Mary's honour) making it her chief aim through life to serve and honour that glorious Mother. Her devotion extended also to St. Joseph, the Virgin Spouse of our Lady, who one day manifested to St. Teresa how well-pleasing his devotion was in her eyes, assuring her of the success of every undertaking placed under his special protection. Teresa was called of God to reform the Carmelite Order, and Mary frequently appeared to encourage, instruct, and guide her; thus it was that Teresa, a poor Virgin, possessing no worldly goods, nor earthly patrons, was able (spite of all the powerful opposition she encountered) to found 32 Convents, in which the Carmelite Rule was observed in its pristine severity. Mary had assured St. Teresa of her own aid and of St. Joseph's prot ction, and the result showed

the fidelity with which this promise was fulfilled. So highly did Teresa appreciate the aid of her celestial mother that she chose her as the Patroness of each new Convent she founded, placing its key at the foot of her image, and entrusting the whole community to Mary's powerful protection. Teresa died at Alba, in Spain, in the year 1582, in the 68th year of her age. Angelic hands bore her soul heavenwards to enjoy eternal bliss in the presence of Jesus and His Blessed Mother. Like St. Teresa, let us love and reverence our celestial Mother; through her dedicate all our undertakings to our Divine Lord; at her hands ask counsel and guidance; trust in her aid with child-like simplicity: so, we too shall be enabled, with St. Teresa, to work mighty works for the glory of our God.

PRACTICE.

Whenever you behold a Crucifix, raise your heart in love to Jesus.

10th DAY.

Mary's Sacrifice.

3rd Part.

1. WITH REGARD TO GOD. As the roseate hues of morn herald in the noon-day brightness, so was it with Mary in her Temple life. She grew in virtue, perfection, and love to her Creator. To please Him was her sole aim, therefore she kept vigilant guard over her every act and thought. How beautiful and sublime was Mary's sanctity! Though but a mere child, her virtues were heroic. Alas for me! I who am so advanced in years, and, it may be, more advanced still in the ways of folly and of sin!

2. WITH REGARD TO HER NEIGHBOUR. As her heart was wholly consumed by divine love, we can easily conceive the ardour with which she urged her young companions onwards in the practice of every virtue. Whilst aiding and encouraging them in all their difficulties her chief aim was to kindle and cherish within their hearts the flames of that same love. Truly, charity is the leading

and noblest characteristic of the followers of Jesus Christ. Is it thy leading trait?—Do thy works testify that thou also art a true follower of thy Divine Lord?

3. WITH REGARD TO HERSELF. What a touching spectacle! A Virgin, and one who had no ground for fear, she nevertheless kept most vigilant watch over every thought and feeling. And thou, frail mortal, art so rash as to expose thy few newly acquired virtues to the greatest danger. Unhappy one! behold the abyss yawning at thy feet, and which must inevitably engulf thee, unless thou art on thy guard and withdrawest speedily from its edge!

PRAYER.

Virgin most venerable, Virgin most renowned, pray for us.

Thy sublime greatness, the splendour of thy virtues, the majesty of thy glory, command our deepest reverence, our most exalted praise. No created being, in Heaven or in earth, can be compared with thee. May every tongue hymn thy praise! May we honour thee in word and deed, imitate thy perfect virtue, and view it as our highest privilege to be counted among the

number of thy faithful servants. This is our most heart-felt desire, and earnest prayer. Amen.

Example.

The Venerable Thomas à Kempis.

The Venerable Thomas à Kempis, to whom, amongst many other writings, we are indebted for the 'Imitation of Christ,' from early childhood entertained a deep affection for the Blessed Virgin. He made a practice of reciting certain prayers and devotions, daily, in her honour. But, during his student-years he had unhappily grown lax in the observance of this practice; neglecting first one devotion, then another, until, as so frequently happens in the days of youth, he omitted them nearly all. Such was his condition, when the following dream happened to him, a dream which we may rightly view as heaven-sent. It seemed to him that as he was in school with his companions, our Lady appeared encircled by indescribable glory and majesty; her countenance radiant, her garments whiter than snow, and more glittering than the sun. He noticed that she conversed with all the monks, conferring on each one some signal mark of her maternal care and love, at the same time expressing her great delight at the pains

they took in training those young souls for whom Jesus, her Divine Son, shed His Blood. In contemplating this extreme kindness on Mary's part, Thomas was filled with an ardent desire and hope that she would also cast her gracious eyes on him, or favour him with some loving words. "Truly, I do not merit such a favour," thought he to himself, "but then I have never ceased to love Mary, and she is such a gracious Mother." Such were his thoughts, but the result showed how greatly he was mistaken! Instead of receiving a token of her affection, he met with a severe rebuke. When the Blessed Virgin came to the place where Thomas was sitting, she gave him a stern look, saying: "It is useless for thee to expect any mark of love from me, for thou hast, by culpable neglect and the deceitful suggestions of a faithless counsellor, ceased to pay me my promised tribute. Where are thy devotional practices? Where thy prayers, thy former works? Has not thy love and devotion to me grown wholly cold? And yet thou art so rash as to expect proofs of my love when I have reason to express my discontent and displeasure! Thou art unworthy of my affection, because thou hast so lightly renounced those practices in which, formerly, thou didst take such delight, and which

thou knewest to be so well-pleasing to me! . . . "
After saying this, the Queen of Heaven disappeared, leaving Thomas in a state of bitter sorrow and deep contrition. This Vision roused him from his lethargy; he acknowledged his fault; promised amendment; and at once recommenced his former devotional exercises, which he observed faithfully unto his dying day. He daily thanked his Celestial Mother for awaking him from his indifference, and receiving him back into her service. He did all in his power to repair his former negligence: he frequently recited the "Ave Maria," for which he had a special devotion, and which he paraphrased in the following beautiful manner:

Whenever I utter the Angelic Salutation, I will do so, O Mary, with feelings of reverence, devotion, and trust. I proffer it to thee, with bent head, with arms outstretched to thee in deepest devotion, desiring ardently that the Angelic Spirits may recite this salutation myriads of times to thy praise. I know of nothing that redounds so much to thine honour, or ministers so much to my own consolation, as this greeting. Let all who love thy most blessed name lend an attentive ear; let Heaven rejoice, and earth be filled with glad surprise when I say: "Hail Mary!" Let Satan

flee, and earth tremble, when I repeat: "Hail, Mary!" Let sadness vanish, and new, sweet joy fill my heart whenever I pray: "Hail, Mary!" my waning love grows strong, my whole soul revives when I exclaim: "Hail, Mary!" My devotion waxes more fervent, my contrition deepens, my hope is strengthened, and fresh consolation inundates my soul so oft as I cry: "Hail, Mary!" So sweet is this greeting, that mortal utterances fail to express its depth. Again do I approach thee, O holiest of Virgins, to greet thee once more: "Hail, Mary!" Who will aid me to praise thee as I would fain desire to do! Would that all my members could be transformed into tongues wherewith to greet thee! Would that my lips might glow with never-ending praise to thee! O most blessed Mother of my God! prostrate in thy presence, penetrated with the deepest devotion and heart-felt joy at the sound of thy holy name, I offer thee the bliss thou didst experience when the Archangel's greeting fell on thy ears. May I with pure lips and glowing heart, ever repeat: "Hail, Mary!"

PRACTICE.

Observe moderation at your meals, remembering that God sees you.

11th Day.

The Annunciation.

1st Part.

Mary was appointed to be the Mother of God. This dignity was a lofty one, in the order of Nature, Grace, and Glory.

1. IN THE ORDER OF NATURE. As true Mother of the Word Incarnate, the Blessed Virgin entered into a relationship with God, far higher and more intimate than can fall to the lot of any other created being. From her was born Jesus Christ, Son of the Eternal, very God and very Man; therefore is she rightly named the Mother of God. An honour this, far exceeding our highest thought. Know, O Christian soul, that Mary, the Mother of thy Redeemer, deigns to be the Mother of sinners also. With child-like trust flee to her, place thyself beneath her protection, and strive to live a life well-pleasing in her eyes.

2. IN THE ORDER OF GRACE. In virtue of her divine maternity, the boundless treasures of

Divine Grace are to a certain degree under Mary's control. As a Son, Jesus was subject to her, obeyed her commands, complied with her slightest wish. With what readiness then must He answer her petitions when she supplicates any favour for us! St. Bernard says, God wills that she who was chosen to be the Mother of the Redeemer should be the channel of every grace won for us by her Divine Son. Why then dost not thou, who art so poor, and lacking in grace, address thyself to this rich, mighty, tender Mother? Entreat her to aid thee, compassionate thy poverty, and enrich thee with an abundant supply of grace.

3. IN THE ORDER OF GLORY. Holy Scripture says of Mary that she is enthroned at her Son's Right Hand, far above all the Angelic Choirs. *The Queen sat on Thy Right Hand.* If eye hath not seen, nor ear heard, nor hath it entered into the heart of man to conceive the glory God has prepared for them that love Him, how far surpassing human comprehension must that glory be which the Holy Trinity has bestowed on the Divine Mother! What joy and consolation for us to know that our Mother and our Heavenly Queen dwells in eternal glory and majesty. Let us so live that we may merit to dwell with her hereafter, gaze on her splendour, proffer her our

congratulations and homage, and participate in her bliss throughout eternity.

PRAYER.

Virgin most powerful, pray for us.

O Virgin, truly mighty art thou in Heaven, Earth, and Hell, inasmuch as Jesus, thy Son, can refuse thee nothing, and has given thee to share, in a certain measure, in His Divine Omnipotence. Thou art the channel through which He aids, succours, and liberates us from all temporal and spiritual danger. The elements own thy power. Thou art the destroyer of all heresy; thou hast crushed the serpent's head and robbed him of his prey. Virgin most mighty, pray for us. Aid and strengthen us against our foes and thine. Give us victory over Satan, and aid us to win eternal life. Amen.

EXAMPLE.

St. Francis Jerome.

The Church celebrates the festival of this Saint (a member of the Society of Jesus) on the 11th of May. He was a truly apostolic man, and was revered as such in Naples. He was also a faithful servant of Mary, for whom he entertained the deep-

est veneration and love, making it his constant aim to inspire others with the same sentiments. It was his constant practice to fast, on bread and water, every Saturday as well as on the Vigils preceding the feasts of our Lady. In the Church of the Jesuits, in Naples, was a picture of the Blessed Virgin, sent from Rome by Saint Francis Borgia, and venerated under the title of *Our Lady, Help of Mothers*, devotion to whom St. Jerome did all in his power to encourage. For the space of twenty-two years he preached every Thursday in one of the Churches dedicated to our Lady, selecting, as his topic, Mary's special privileges and the innumerable graces which fall to the lot of her true clients. He was extremely zealous in promulgating devotion to Mary among the young, considering it the most potent means of shielding their innocence and reclaiming the wanderer. He was wont to say that it was a difficult matter for any to attain true holiness who were lacking in devotion to our Lady. In the hour of doubt, or anxiety, Mary was his counsellor, his support in all his undertakings, his refuge in danger, and his strong fortress. Never had he recourse to her without obtaining relief. When on his missions, he always had a picture of the Blessed Virgin placed in view of his auditors, that he might, by her intercession,

ensure the Divine blessing on his labours, and lead his hearers to Jesus through Mary. It is astonishing how much good this apostolic man effected under Mary's protection, how many souls he won. Whatever the sphere of his labours, a marked increase in devotion to the Blessed Virgin was the unfailing result. His services were not left unrewarded by the Mother of Mercy; after protecting him through life, she was his shield in the hour of death. He died in Naples in the year 1716; was beatified by Pope Pius VII. in the year 1806, and canonized on the 29th of May, 1839, by Pope Gregory XVI. Let us learn from St. Jerome how good it is to love and honour Mary, and share his conviction that it is difficult to attain holiness unless we truly honour Mary.

PRACTICE.

To testify your love to Jesus and Mary, deny yourself something at your meals.

12TH DAY.

THE ANNUNCIATION.

2ND PART.

The advantages enjoyed by Mary, as regarded body, heart, and mind.

1. MARY'S PHYSICAL SUPERIORITY. As the chosen Mother of the Word Incarnate, Mary was physically superior to all other creatures. Apart from those perfections, in virtue of which the Archangel Gabriel saluted her as blessed, Mary was the first to unfurl the standard of Virginity and dedicate her person to the Lord. How well-pleasing such purity must have been in the eyes of Him *who delights Himself among the lilies!* How displeasing to Him must be the impurity that stains so many a soul, and perchance thine also!

2. MARY'S HEART WAS A TREASURY OF PERFECTION. Her perfect purity, sanctity, and her extreme humility, which enhanced the lustre of those virtues, were well-pleasing in the Divine

Sight. The Angel announced to her that she should become the Mother of God; she gives herself no other title than that of a lowly, obedient servant: *Behold the handmaid of the Lord.*

Hardly has she uttered these words, when He, who never despises the lowly heart, descended from Heaven to take upon Himself the flesh of that pure Virgin, and, for our sakes, become man. Bear in mind that God abhors the proud, but takes delight in the meek and lowly.

3. THE SPIRIT WHICH ANIMATED MARY. If any one had power to expedite the Messiah's Advent, certainly that person was Mary. As head of the faithful, and replete with the fulness of grace, by the might of her faith, by the ardour of her earnest desires and heartfelt prayers, Mary drew the Eternal Word down from Heaven to become Incarnate in her Virgin-womb. Let your faith be a living practical faith; have your neighbour's spiritual welfare at heart; earnestly pray for the conversion of sinners; so shall your supplications be abundantly answered; and your merits greatly augmented.

PRAYER.

Virgin most merciful, pray for us.

O Virgin, replete with that love and mercy

with which God, the fount of all goodness, so richly endowed thee, especially during the time that He tarried within thy womb, never has thy compassionate heart rejected a sinner (however great the magnitude of his crimes), who turned to thee with truly contrite heart. Heaven and Earth are full of the tokens of thy goodness and mercy. This it is which encourages us to confide in thee. Have pity on us; compassionate our misery, O merciful Virgin; pray for us; save us. Amen.

Example.

St. Alphonsus Liguori.

St. Alphonsus Liguori, canonized on the 29th of May, 1839, was a most zealous and devout child of Mary, and one of the most saintly Prelates who have adorned the Church in these latter days. Nothing can afford us a clearer proof of the degree of holiness attained by him than the testimony of those who knew him intimately, and who unanimously assert that no stain ever sullied his baptismal robe of innocence. This privilege he owed to his deep, tender veneration for the Blessèd Virgin, to whose service he had consecrated himself in a special manner. From his earliest years Mary was the object of his

tenderest affection, a sentiment which waxed ever stronger and stronger with each advancing year. She was the object of his most filial veneration and child-like trust; to her he had recourse in every need, in every danger, fully assured that never would Mary fail him. He sought to inspire others with the same degree of confidence; and never wearied of reminding them that to Mary as well as to Jesus, the world owes its Redemption; that if Jesus is the fount, she is the channel of every grace. He loved to hymn her praise, not only in his sermons but in his writings, and richly did our Lady reward her faithful client. At the close of life he told a priest that he ever sought counsel from Mary in all his undertakings, and specially so in everything connected with the *Confraternity of the Redeemer* (which owed its foundation to our saint), adding that Mary had imparted many wondrous things to him. To this fact must be atttibuted the deep pathos and impassioned words in which the prayers and hymns abound, penned by him in Mary's honour. During his missions he spoke with such unction and fervour of Mary's lofty privileges, that crowds thronged to listen to him, and many a hardened sinner was converted.

We will here cite a few of the devotions practised by him in her honour. He never passed

a single day without reciting his prayers before our Lady's image. On Saturdays and the Vigils of her Feasts, he fasted on bread and water. It was his daily practice to visit a Church or Chapel dedicated to Mary. He wore her scapular, and also a chaplet, round his neck, and together with the members of his confraternity, had another rosary hanging from his girdle. There was a large picture of our Lady, hanging in his room, to which he often directed his loving gaze, in order to salute her, or beg some favour at her hands. He recited the chaplet daily, devoutly meditating on the different mysteries. He also said the five Psalms in honour of Mary's name, reciting an Ave Maria every quarter of an hour, even when others were with him; he never failed to say the Hail Mary, morning, noon, and night; and if passing through the street when the Angelus sounded, would kneel down upon the ground; he did this even when he was bishop. On leaving the house, he first committed himself to Mary's protection, and never failed to salute her on returning home. On Saturdays he was wont to choose Mary's exalted virtues as the special theme of his discourse, and desired this practice should be observed in all the houses of the Confraternity. May we imitate this devout servant of Mary so

far as in us lies! What graces and blessings may we not then hope for from Mary.

Practice.

From time to time, awake within your breast, Hope and Love.

13th Day.

The Annunciation.

3rd Part.

Fruits of the Incarnation: as regards God, as regards Mary, and as regards ourselves.

1. AS REGARDS GOD. The Incarnation and birth of the Eternal Word contributed to augment the glory of God; until then, God had no other subjects save creatures of limited intelligence, and greatly lacking in perfection; after the Nativity of Christ, God's Kingdom was enriched by a subject of boundless worth and unlimited perfection. He who formerly spoke of Himself as the God of Abraham, Isaac, and Jacob, could now speak of Himself as the God of an Incarnate God.

How stands it with thee, O Christian? What hast thou done to contribute to the Divine Glory? Hast thou, by thy godly life, conversation, and edifying example, led souls to Christ; or by thy careless, unchristian behaviour, seduced them from His service?

2. AS REGARDS MARY HERSELF. The Blessed Virgin beheld a God obedient to her commands, as a child is subject to its mother. What an honour was this for Mary!—And thou, who contemplatest this humiliation on the part of God, this exaltation of Mary, how dost thou fulfil thy filial duties? Art thou obedient as Jesus was to his Mother? On the contrary, dost thou not chafe at submitting to the yoke of obedience?

3. AS REGARDS OURSELVES. Mary is the Mother of God; she also deigns to be the contrite sinner's Mother, and, as the Mother of the Divine Judge, intercedes with Him on our behalf. What can such a loving son refuse His mother? Flee then to Mary, O my soul, beseech her to take pity on thee, and secure thy salvation, which cost her Son so dear, and which is so dear to her maternal heart! Be assured that all will be well with thee if thou art not lacking in true devotion and love to Mary. Amen.

PRAYER.

Virgin, most faithful, pray for us!

O Virgin, constant in thy fidelity to God, whose will thou didst perfectly fulfil; ever-faithful to Jesus, thy Son, between whom and thyself so close

a union subsisted that nought on earth could sever it, ever-faithful to such as invoke thy aid, obtain us pardon for our want of fidelity to God. Win us grace that we may, for the future, be stedfast in serving Him, and, after thy example, lend a ready ear to His inspirations, faithfully observe the devotions instituted in honour of thy Divine Son and of thyself, and, in virtue of our fidelity to Him, may we be admitted hereafter into His Celestial Kingdom.

EXAMPLE.

St. Bernard.

St. Bernard, the first abbot of Clairvaux, was an ornament and pillar of the Church in the twelfth century. By his impressive eloquence, apostolic zeal, and the sanctity of his life, he did much to promote the honour of God. His devotion and love to the Blessed Virgin are both striking and edifying. One cannot peruse the prayers and discourses he composed in Mary's honour, without experiencing feelings of the deepest emotion. From childhood, Bernard had chosen Mary as his patroness, and on many occasions the Mother of Mercy testified how pleasing to her was the devotion he cherished for her, and how deeply

she interested herself in his salvation. Whilst he was a mere child Mary appeared to him one Christmas night, in company with her Divine Son, and disclosed to him the whole mystery of the Nativity. This kindled within his breast the flames of never-dying love, and gave rise to a magnificent work in praise of Jesus and His Divine Mother, which he completed later on. Bernard received many proofs of Mary's love. Amongst others, she appeared to him during an illness, which the doctors pronounced incurable, laid her hand on him, healing him at once. Bernard strove to render others participators of his own ardent love for the Queen of Heaven. In order to stimulate confidence in her, he was wont to say: "She lacks not power, for she is the Mother of God; she lacks not good-will, for she is the Mother of Mercy and our Mother; and not only is she the Mother of the righteous, but the poor sinner's Mother also". Well may we style St. Bernard Mary's panegyrist, for, among all the Holy Fathers and Doctors of the Church, no one has written or spoken so eloquently and impressively in Mary's glory as St. Bernard has done. So long as the world lasts, his writings will proclaim Mary's praise and fan the flames of love within the Christian's heart. He died at the age of 62, in the

year of grace, 1153, and was interred in front of our Lady's Altar, the altar of her whom through life he had loved so tenderly and honoured so deeply. The following short prayer, written in honour of our Lady, is extracted from the Saint's writings:

O Blessed Mother! Thou art the Mother of God, the Mother of sinners, the Mother of the banished ones! Grant, Oh gracious Virgin, that I, thy sinful child, may not be condemned by thy Divine Son, but do thou intercede for me, that He, the Divine Judge, may at last welcome me, a poor exile, into the Eternal Home. Amen.

PRACTICE.

Every evening, carefully examine your conscience.

14th Day.

The Visitation.

1st Part.

In the Visitation, three things claim our attention: the motive which animated our Lady; the difficulties of the journey; and the promptitude with which she accomplished it.

1. THE MOTIVE. This was nothing less than the most ardent desire to bring joy and benediction to Elizabeth's roof, and co-operate with her Son in effecting man's redemption. Mary might easily have remained at home quietly praising God who had done such great things for her. But as the salvation of souls was in question, souls for whom the Son of God had just become incarnate within her Virgin womb, she arises at once; quits her quiet, contemplative life, to proceed to the spot where the voice of love calls her. Thus does Mary teach thee by her own example how at times thou too must leave God in order to render thy neighbour service.

2. THE FATIGUES AND DIFFICULTIES OF THE JOURNEY. In spite of the weakness of her sex and the delicacy of her frame, the Blessed Virgin

undertook the journey to Hebron, a town some distance from Nazareth, the road to which was a mountainous one, and one of much difficulty. But love lent Mary courage, energy, and strength. Compare thy conduct with her's, and when thou notest how ready thou art to let the slightest obstacle be an excuse for not coming to thy neighbour's assistance, be sure that thou lackest charity, and art spiritually dead.

3. THE PROMPTITUDE WITH WHICH OUR BLESSED LADY UNDERTOOK THE JOURNEY. The Gospel says expressly: *Mary arose and went to the hill country in haste.* Why so? Jesus intended to sanctify his forerunner John; therefore Mary hastened to accomplish the will of her Divine Son and carry out His mission regarding John, as speedily as possible. The Holy Ghost is impatient of all delay and procrastination; the spirit of idleness, laziness, and procrastination has certainly not its origin in God. Prove thyself in this respect, and follow the inspirations of the Holy Spirit; but do so without the least delay.

PRAYER.

Mirror of justice, pray for us.

O Mary, every Christian virtue is reflected in

thee. No shadow, dimness, or blemish sullies thy brilliancy; thou shinest with the fulness of every grace. Copying thy Divine Son, thy desire was to fulfil all righteousness. In this mirror we will often gaze; thy holiness shall ever be before our eyes, so that we may learn from thee how to regulate our life and conduct. Obtain us pardon for our unrighteous deeds; intercede with God that He may grant us grace to walk in the paths of righteousness and persevere unto the end, so that through all Eternity we may enjoy the fulness of His Mercy. Amen.

EXAMPLE.

St. Francis Borgia.

Among those Saints who have been the Blessed Virgin's most zealous champions, St. Francis Borgia (Duke of Candia, and afterwards General of the Society of Jesus), stands pre-eminently forth. He lived a pious life when in the world; but God, having destined him for a high degree of sanctity, drew him closer to Himself, and that in the following manner. When Isabella, wife of Charles V., died at Toledo, in the bloom of youth, our Saint was entrusted with the honourable task of conveying the corpse to

Granada, the usual place of interment for the royal house of Spain. Before handing over the corpse to the ecclesiastical authorities of Granada, it was necessary that Francis should swear to its identity. But on opening the coffin the face of the deceased was found so disfigured that not a trace of her features was discernible. At the sight of such a mass of corruption, a ray of grace penetrated our saint's soul; that corpse was to him a picture of all earthly grandeur and terrestrial bliss. Scarcely had he re-entered his own dwelling than he threw himself on his knees, spent the whole night in prayer, tears, and sighs, making the following vow: *Lord, never more will I serve any being of whom death can rob me.* After his wife's death he faithfully carried out this resolve, and, renouncing all worldly honours and possessions, entered the Society of Jesus, in order to serve God in humility and retirement. Throughout the whole course of his life he was animated by the deepest love for our Blessed Lady. He daily observed several devotional practices in her honour; foremost among them was the Rosary, the mysteries of which, in accordance with the spirit of the Church, he meditated devoutly upon; and whenever our Lord's Incarnation, Life, or Sufferings formed the subject of

his contemplation, he invariably turned his eyes to her who was so intimately associated with these mysteries. When meditating on the Incarnation, he pictured our Lord in His Virgin Mother's womb; at the mysteries of His Birth and Infancy he pictured the Redeemer in His Divine Mother's arms; at His hidden life, he beheld Jesus subject to Mary; in meditating on His Ministry, he called to mind the attention with which Mary listened to Jesus, treasuring all His words in her heart; when our Divine Lord's sufferings were his theme, he pictured the sorrowful Mother's heart transfixed by the sword of grief. His constant aim was to awake within his own breast the sorrows which fell to Mary's share. Thus, in all his meditations on the mystery of the Redemption, his gaze was riveted on her who so lovingly and heroically co-operated in effecting our salvation. The boundless confidence he placed in Jesus as our Redeemer and Mediator, was extended to Mary, whom he regarded as our advocate with her Divine Son. These sentiments he strove to impart to others, both by his lip and pen. Not only was he anxious to win Mary adherents from among the people, he also introduced this devotion into the houses of the rich and great, thereby reclaiming sinners, strengthening the weak, and leading many on the

road to perfection. Fully persuaded that none ever prayed in vain who came to Jesus by Mary, he always had recourse to her, finding help and consolation, and that often in the most marvellous manner. So true it is that Mary never forsakes her faithful clients, and that, as St. Bernard says, none ever approach this Mother of Mercy, with humble trusting heart, without obtaining relief.

Practice.

Be merciful to the poor; if thou hast much, give of thy abundance, if thou hast little, be diligent to give of that little for Jesus' sake.

15TH DAY.

THE VISITATION.

2ND PART.

Note Mary's discretion, her conversation, and the result of her visit.

1. MARY'S DISCRETION. Note Mary's discretion, humility, and reserve. In describing this mystery the Evangelist draws attention to the reverent and unassuming manner in which the Blessed Virgin greets her cousin Elizabeth: he does so in order that we may observe the discretion which characterized Zachariah's family. Never forget that discreet modesty and reserve are the leading traits of a truly Christian soul.

2. HER CONVERSATION. As St. Bonaventura remarks, Mary related to her cousin the whole story of the Incarnation; and Elizabeth, in return, narrated how she, who had so long been barren, had conceived in her old age. Such discourse inflamed their hearts with burning love to God. How is it with you? What are your favourite

topics? Do they resemble Mary's, or rather, do you not waste your time in idle, unkind, and uncharitable remarks? Resolve to amend; bridle your tongue; and let your lips utter nought save that which is edifying, calculated to promote the glory of God, and advance your own salvation.

3. THE RESULTS OF THIS VISIT. At the moment Mary crossed the threshold of Elizabeth's dwelling John was sanctified, whilst yet in his mother's womb, and, together with his mother, received the full outpouring of the Holy Ghost; also we can truly say that it was by Mary's instrumentality that Zachariah recovered the use of speech. O blessèd home that, under whose roof Mary enters! Invoke her, O Christian soul, that thy soul may be sanctified as was John's, thy heart glow with ardent love as did Elizabeth's, thy tongue be loosed, that with Zachariah thou mayest henceforth glorify thy God.

PRAYER.

Seat of Wisdom, pray for us!

O Mary, truly art thou the seat of Wisdom, for the Son of God, the eternal Wisdom of the Father, reposed in thine arms and on thy Virgin-breast, and

filled thee with the plentitude of wisdom. Rightly does the Church style thee the Seat of Wisdom. But we, poor sinners, wander on in darkness and the shadow of death, knowing not what is really for our good! Intercede for us, good Mother, that we may receive the gift of wisdom and love, and strive after all that will make us well-pleasing in the Divine Sight, and fit us for eternal bliss. Amen.

EXAMPLE.

The Servite Fathers.—St. Philip Benitus.

Early in the 13th Century there lived in Florence seven men, rich and of noble birth, distinguished for their zeal in God's service, and for their devotion to the Virgin Mother. These persons felt themselves simultaneously moved to withdraw wholly from the world, in order that they might, in the quiet of retirement and beneath Mary's protection, do penance for the sins of the world, and supplicate pardon for the transgressors. Such was the origin of the celebrated order of the Servants of Mary, or Servites, so called because the chief aim of its members is to render special honour to the Blessed Virgin. This order, so worthy of esteem, not only on account of the name it bears, but for the many services it has

rendered the Church, owes its increase and prosperity, in a great measure, to the efforts of St. Philip Benitus, who, soon after the founding of the Order, was enrolled among its members, and, later on, elected General of the same.

Philip was only five months old when he first beheld the seven founders, who were collecting alms; suddenly, his tongue was loosed, and turning to his mother, he exclaimed: "Behold the servants of Mary". This miracle gave rise to the title assumed by the Order.

When in his fifteenth year, Philip began to reflect as to his future vocation, praying earnestly, especially to our Blessed Lady, for light and guidance. At the reading of the Epistle one day when in the Servite Church, he felt himself inwardly called to join the Order. In order to discern the Will of God more clearly, he addressed himself with redoubled fervour to Mary, and in the following night received a fresh token of the Divine Will, to the same effect as before; thus persuaded what the Will of God concerning him was, he hastened on the morrow to the Superior, and kneeling down, humbly asked admission into the Order. His prayer was granted, and Philip now consecrated himself wholly to Mary's service, striving to win the approbation of the Queen of Heaven by

holiness of life and imitation of her exalted virtues. From a spirit of obedience, he allowed himself, later on, to be consecrated Priest, and with apostolic zeal at once began to preach the Gospel, exhorting sinners to repentance. Under Mary's protection his preaching was crowned with marvellous success; his constant aim was to promulgate devotion to the seven Dolours of our Lady, in order to move sinners to repentance and encourage Christian souls in the paths of virtue.

After a life marked by the greatest purity of heart and spirit, and the practice of the most exalted virtues, the moment at last approached when he was to receive the reward of his labours. On the Feast of the Assumption he was seized with violent fever, passed the Octave of the Feast in acts of ardent love to God, of tenderest devotion to Mary, and of the deepest contrition for his own sins. On the final day of the Octave he received the Holy Viaticum, after which he fell into a death-like swoon. When this had lasted three hours, and each moment was thought to be his last, he suddenly recovered consciousness, and addressing himself to the bystanders, told them that Satan had done his utmost to plunge him in perdition, but that the Blessed Virgin had delivered him from all dangers. Hereupon he

asked for his book (thus he named his Crucifix), and fixing his eyes on the Crucified, and invoking Jesus and Mary, gave up the ghost, on the 22nd of August, 1285. May we too strain every nerve to serve Mary worthily, and esteem it our highest privilege so to do! Then may we count with certainty on her aid, especially in the hour of death.

Practice.

Frequently make some little act of mortification; and if you do no more, bridle your tongue, and keep strict watch over your eyes.

16th Day.

The Visitation.

3rd Part.

Mary spent three months with her cousin: note three things, —the advantages accruing to St. John; the comfort this visit was to his mother Elizabeth; and the edification resulting therefrom, as regarded Zachariah's household.

1. The advantages, as regards St. John. Mary remained three months with her cousin Elizabeth. If at her mere salutation and entrance into the house John was sanctified in his mother's womb, what graces must he not have received in virtue of her long sojourn, her prayers and heroic virtues! What wonder that John became a Saint, and that among the children of men there was none like unto him! Happy the parents who dedicate their offspring to Mary, even before their birth! Learn from her how zealously thou shouldst guard the innocence of youth, and lead them on in virtue's paths. Usually, a man's future character is the result of his early training.

2. THE COMFORT TO ELIZABETH. What delight and joy Mary's visit to her cousin must have been! We might picture this in some faint degree, could we comprehend what it is to dwell three months with her who is the joy of the Elect, and the bliss of Heaven. In thy hours of suffering and weariness, why dost thou not flee to her whom Holy Church terms, "Comforter of the Afflicted, and Help of Christians"?

3. THE BENEFICIAL RESULTS, AS REGARDED ZACHARIAH'S HOUSEHOLD. Mary fulfilled the lowliest tasks in her cousin's family; and this with the greatest alacrity, cheerfulness, humility, and love. Though the Blessed Mother of the Redeemer, she put her hand to every species of house-work, omitting no opportunity of doing good and ministering to the happiness of her neighbours. What an example to Zachariah's family! What an example to thee also, thou who art so slow and unwilling to aid *thy* neighbour; so tenacious of thy own opinion, and so inflated with pride!

PRAYER.

Cause of our joy, pray for us!

O Mary, thou art the cause of our joy, in life, in death, and throughout Eternity. Thou didst

introduce this joy on earth when thou gavest birth to our Redeemer and our Saviour. Thou nourishest this joy within our hearts, by aiding us in our varied needs and answering all who invoke thee with filial trust. Thou wilt perfect this joy, when, as we confidently hope, thou wilt shield and succour us in the hour of death, and introduce us to Eternal Life. Mother of Mercy! forsake us not in temptation's hour; strengthen our hope in thee and in thy Son. Never allow our courage to languish, but cheer us with thine aid, make us patient under suffering, and render our wills conformable to the Will of thy Divine Son. Amen.

EXAMPLE.

St. Francis of Sales.

Through the whole course of his life St. Francis of Sales was conspicuous for his deep love and devotion to the Blessed Mother of God, from whom he received many extraordinary favours. We cite one instance proving his childlike trust in Mary, and Mary's tender care for her faithful servant. The Saint was pursuing his studies in Paris, and leading a pious, virtuous life. By the Divine permission, the gravest doubts as to his eternal salvation took possession of his mind, so

that he wholly despaired of ever beholding the Beatific Vision. It is easy to imagine the deep impression such thoughts made on one who loved God with so ardent an affection, and who longed so intensely to be joined to Him in closest union. This temptation deprived him of all peace of mind; day and night he was haunted by the same terrific thoughts; his bodily and mental strength gave way; he grew pale and thin, and grave doubts were entertained as to his restoration to health.

During this period of intense mental suffering he had constant recourse to Him who is the God of all consolation; and one day when the temptation was stronger than usual, so that he knew not how to bear it, he flew to the Church where he had formerly taken the vow of chastity. The first object that met his gaze was an image of the Blessed Mother of God; this sight was as healing balsam to his wounded heart. His wonted confidence in Mary received new life and force. He threw himself on his knees, and conscious of his own unworthiness to approach Him whose presence he might never enjoy, he earnestly entreated Mary to obtain for him one favour, viz., that if destined to eternal perdition, God would at least grant him grace to love and glorify Him to the utmost of his powers throughout the whole course

of his mortal life. In order to secure a more favourable hearing, he recited the *Memorare*, with heartfelt devotion, and burst into a flood of tears. The Mother of Mercy could not turn a deaf ear to such a petition as this. In a single moment all his doubts vanished; his peace of mind was restored; and the deepest confidence filled his soul with joy unspeakable. His health and colour returned at once, so that not the slightest vestige of his former suffering was discernible in his countenance. From that time the deepest peace, the peace of God that passeth understanding, inundated his breast; no cloud ever marred its serenity; and the remembrance of Mary's goodness to him on this occasion was, throughout the whole course of his life, a lasting incentive to place the deepest trust in her and love her with his whole heart.

Practice.

On retiring to rest, remember the hour of death, and that perchance you may never see the morrow's sun.

17TH DAY.

THE PURIFICATION OF THE BLESSED VIRGIN.

1ST PART.

In this mystery, Mary is a model of obedience; the act of obedience she practised involved suffering on Mary's part; her obedience was blind and magnanimous.

1. THE CIRCUMSTANCES WHICH RENDERED THIS ACT SO TRYING. It was prescribed in the Law that all women should, at a stated time after childbirth, repair to the Temple and present themselves to the priest in order that they might be purified. By complying with this precept they virtually acknowledged their own uncleanness in the eye of the law. Therefore such a ceremony must have been a very trying ordeal to Mary, the purest of Virgins; nevertheless, she fulfilled the law to the very utmost. Does not her example fill thee with confusion, who art so prone to murmur at having to comply with anything that is in the least degree distasteful to thy feelings?

2. **The perfection and blindness of Mary's obedience.** The precept regarding purification after child-birth only affected those who had conceived and given birth to offspring in accordance with the general laws of nature. But Mary had conceived her Divine Son by the power of the Holy Ghost. Yet she does not plead this as an excuse, but obeys the law in its entirety, although such a law was not applicable in her case. But thou, how often dost thou not seek to dispense thyself from obeying the divine precepts, and those of the Church, which it is strictly incumbent on thee to fulfil. Deep shame must overwhelm thee when thou comparest thy conduct with that of Mary.

3. **Mary's magnanimity.** Mary fulfilled even the minutest precept of the Law, and this in the most perfect manner. In doing more than it was compulsory on her to do, she evinced her liberality and generosity to God's word and gave a striking proof of the depths of her love for Him. And thou, how niggardly art thou towards thy God. Thou wilt do only just so much as thou art obliged; and that little is but imperfectly done. Remember that God loveth a cheerful giver, and that he who giveth abundantly, shall be rewarded in the same degree.

Prayer.

Spiritual Vessel, Vessel of honour, pray for us.

O Blessed Virgin, rightly dost thou merit these titles, for the Lord has filled thy heart with the costliest gifts of the Holy Ghost. Thy thoughts were ever noble and lofty, thy sentiments holy, thy intentions sublime and pure. Thy one aim was to glorify thy Creator; He was the sole object of thy love and thy desire. The richest, noblest gifts of nature, grace, and glory, were lavished on thee in the richest abundance. But we, poor mortals, are nought save vessels of corruption and misery. Gracious, loving Mother, do thou and thy Son have pity on us; commend and present us to Him, that through thy intercession we may share His endless merits, and seek nothing save those things which are holy and eternal. Amen.

Example.

St. Francis Regis.

If devotion to the Blessed Mother of God is profitable and advantageous in all ranks and conditions of life, it is specially so as regards the young. Not only does it inspire their tender

hearts with a lively abhorrence of all evil, it also shows them, in this mirror of righteousness, the true worth and majesty of virtue and sanctity, and assures them of the protection of this gracious, powerful Virgin and Mother. Among those who have experienced the truth of this, John Francis Regis stands pre-eminently forth. This Saint was born in the year 1597, in the diocese of Narbonne, in France. He was of distinguished birth. With his mother's milk he had imbibed the tenderest love to the Divine Mother. And in order to cherish and augment this affection, when still a boy, he hastened to join one of the confraternities founded in Mary's honour. So soon as his wish was fulfilled, he considered himself obliged to lead a life of greater sanctity than before. No one strove more zealously to carry out the aim of the confraternity than Francis did. He multiplied his prayers and devotional practices; communicated more frequently; and redoubled his efforts to render himself more perfect and acceptable in the sight of God and His Blessed Mother. On his admission into the Society of Jesus, his devotion received a fresh impulse. As a teacher, he embraced every opportunity to kindle within the hearts of his pupils a deep love for her who was the object of his own ardent affection. But it was

chiefly during the missions to which he so heroically dedicated the last ten years of his life, that his devotion to Mary was so marked, and that he strove to awake the same feeling in the hearts of the faithful. At the commencement of his apostolic career he placed himself under Mary's powerful protection; her name was ever on his lips, his zeal in her cause was unwearying. In every danger she was his tower of refuge. His instructions, exhortations, and all his sacred labours he commended to her maternal care. In reward for his untiring zeal in winning souls for Christ, and for his deep love and fidelity to Mary, he was accounted worthy of being aided in his dying moments by Jesus and His Blessed Mother, and of being conducted by them to Heaven. So enraptured was he at the sight, that he exclaimed joyously to his comrades: *I see Jesus and Mary coming to meet me, in order to introduce me into the home of the Blessed. Ah, Brother, what happiness! How contented I am to depart!* Saying thus, he gave up the Ghost. Truly it is a blessed thing to die with Jesus and His Blessed Mother standing by. But such a happiness as this none can hope to enjoy save those who have served Jesus and Mary zealously in the days of their life.

PRACTICE.

During the day, repeat the Angelus, or some other prayer, in Mary's honour.

18TH DAY.

THE PURIFICATION.

2ND PART.

Mary was a model of the deepest humility; she shrouded her virginity, sanctity, and divine Motherhood with the veil of the deepest secrecy.

1. HER VIRGINITY. In presenting herself in the Temple to fulfil the law regarding the purification, Mary acted as did those women who were regarded as stained with impurity in the eye of the law. Thus she consented to appear less pure than she really was. O wondrous humility on Mary's part! exclaims St. Vincent Ferrar. "O detestable pride on ours, we, whose desire it is to appear better than we really are!"

2. HER SANCTITY. The same Saint remarks that Mary knelt before the Priest, begging him to intercede on her behalf. The holiest, purest of creatures went so far as to humble herself before a sinful man, content to be regarded as a sinner. And I, the vilest of the vile, why do I persist to pass for good and virtuous in order to win human

applause, thus rendering my condemnation the greater.

3. HER DIVINE MATERNITY. She who gave birth to the Incarnate God could have incurred no stain of guilt thereby. But, as she bore the outward semblance of the daughters of Eve, she desired to conceal her Divine Maternity from mortal eyes. Such humility was well-pleasing in the Divine Sight, and therefore all generations shall call her blessed. Do we desire to honour and imitate our Blessed Lady? Let us at once begin to practise humility, without the possession of which we shall be displeasing in her eyes, and in those of her Divine Son. Let us guard against ostentatious humility; rather let our aim be to practise virtue in all simplicity and sincerity in God's sight, concealing our good deeds from human ken.

PRAYER.

Vessel of singular devotion, pray for us!

Who ever equalled thee in virtue, O most exalted Virgin! Who so devout, who so constant, and untiring in zeal for God's glory? Nought ever marred the union subsisting between thy Creator and thyself; thou wert constant in the performance of duty; the severest trials did but

augment thy virtues and thy merits. Have pity; succour us to overcome our inconstancy, and the slothfulness, alas! so habitual to us! Vessel of singular devotion, pray for us, that our hearts may glow with fervent devotion and ardent zeal; that we may glorify God as we ought, and love Him in time, and eternity. Amen.

Example.

St. Vincent Ferrar.

This Saint, so celebrated in the Church's annals, on account of his eminent sanctity, ardent zeal, and the numerous souls converted by his ministry, was distinguished from earliest childhood by his tender love and devotion to the Blessed Virgin. He strove to the utmost to copy her virtues, and please her by his great purity of heart. Satan seemed to have a certain presentiment of the vast good this faithful servant of Mary would effect; and in order to hinder the same, did his utmost to seduce him from the paths of virtue and plunge him into despair. But our Saint constantly betook himself to his exalted protectress, and by her aid escaped the snares of the enemy. One day, while reading St. Jerome's treatise on the perpetual virginity of Mary, he felt his heart so glow with love

for this virtue, that he prostrated himself on the ground, entreating the Blessed Virgin with his whole heart to preserve his purity ever unsullied. Hardly had he ended his petition, than he heard a voice, saying: Virginity is a rare virtue, it is a grace conferred on but few, and thou must not imagine thyself among that number. Even if thou hast preserved thy chastity unsullied until now, I do not guarantee that thou wilt continue so to do! The alarm these words caused him is almost indescribable, for he had felt convinced Mary would reject none who came to her with a like petition, seeing that purity was so dear to her. He therefore went on praying with redoubled fervour, and soon the Queen of Heaven, radiant with celestial glory, appeared to him, and said: Fear not, my son! What you have just heard is from the lips of the Father of Lies, whose sole motive was to alarm and discourage thee. Be of good cheer, be steadfast in thy resolve, and keep the promises thou hast made. Trust wholly to my Son's mercy, and my own maternal protection. Satan will beset thee with many a temptation; but, by the aid of Divine Grace, thou wilt surmount them all. After saying this, the Blessed Virgin disappeared, and our Saint felt himself inspired by a zeal and courage, the ardour

of which no danger could quench. After this vision St. Vincent led the life of an Angel rather than of a man, advancing daily in the paths of virtue and Christian perfection. Perchance thou too, O reader! hast a violent struggle to endure; it may be that the evil one is striving to rob thy heart of its purity. But fear not; be steadfast and courageous; remember what our Blessed Lady said to St. Vincent; flee to Jesus and Mary, strive manfully, and thou too shalt resist all temptations, and receive an everlasting recompense for thy fidelity. "Blessed are the pure in heart, for they shall see God."

Practice.

Do thy neighbour some service; show him some kindness, for Mary's sake.

19th Day.

The Purification.

3rd Part.

Mary was a model of most ardent love; this love was evinced by her offering her Son in the Temple, ransoming Him, and taking Him home.

1. MARY'S OBLATION OF HER SON. Truly had Mary nought on earth so dear as Jesus, her only Son. And this dearly beloved Son was heroically offered up by her in the Temple, unreservedly and entirely. Not as a mere ceremony did she offer Him, as the other mothers did their offspring, but she offered Him up in the fullest signification of the word, in order that He might suffer and die for us, and fulfil all that the Prophets had foretold concerning Him. In contemplating this Mystery, reflect, O Christian soul, and see what it is thy God demands of thee; truly, it is nought less than the dearest treasure, thine heart: *My son, give me thy heart.* Hitherto thou hast lavished thy affections on the creature, and withdrawn them from Him who so ardently desires to possess them.

What confusion this should awake within thee, who thus insultest Him to whom thou owest all!

2. MARY REDEEMS HER SON. In compliance with the law, Mary redeemed her Son for five pieces of silver. How joyfully she paid that sum, in order to repossess her Son Jesus! What wilt thou give in order to possess Him? Ungrateful one! often thou refusest Him the most trifling alms when He entreats thee for aid by the lips of the poor and needy!

On this occasion, especially, when Mary took her Child back home, she could not desist from lavishing on Him the most abundant proofs of her maternal love. At times she carried Him pressed closely to her Virgin-breast, at other times she handed Him to St. Joseph, that he too might have part in her joy and consolation. Would to God thy love were as ardent, thy zeal as fervent, thy devotion as deep, as Mary's was! At least strive to rouse the most glowing affection within thy heart when thou receivest Him in the Blessed Eucharist, that thou mayest know how to profit to the fullest degree by His gracious Presence.

PRAYER.

Mystical Rose, pray for us!

Mother most amiable! By thy beauty and

unsullied purity, thou wast ever attractive in the Divine Sight; the earth is full of the sweet aroma of thy virtues and of thy perfections, thou art indeed the Mystical Rose, thornless, and welcoming, refreshing all by thy beauty. Entreat Jesus that He would grant us grace to love Him more and more fervently, and that, by our purity and innocence of life, we may spread abroad the sweet odours of Jesus Christ, and daily become more acceptable in His Sight.

EXAMPLE.

The Scapular.—St. Simon Stock.

The origin of the Scapular is attributed to St. Simon, General of the Carmelite Order. English by birth, this servant of God, at the inspiration of the Holy Ghost, withdrew into a desert when twelve years old, in order to devote himself wholly to the contemplation of divine things. His dwelling consisted of a hollow oak tree: hence his name of Stock (which in German means wood, or stick). His time was spent in prayer, fasting, mortification, and other corporal austerities; he drank nothing but water, and lived on the roots and herbs growing in his solitude. Meanwhile the love for Mary, which had

distinguished him from his childhood, grew ever deeper and deeper. He had spent twenty years in this life of penance when the Carmelites arrived in England, in order to introduce their Order there.

Struck by the penitential, remarkable life led by these pious solitaries, and especially impressed by their love and devotion to our Blessed Lady, Simon was induced to join their Order, in which he became a model of zeal and monastic discipline. Later on he was elected General of the Order, and made it his chief aim to animate it more and more with love to Mary, and to augment the fervour of devotion to her in the breasts of the faithful. He often addressed himself to Mary, begging her to show him in what way he could best advance her honour. One day, when praying to this effect before her image, the Celestial Queen appeared, surrounded by a multitude of Angels. She handed him the Scapular, saying that this dress was a proof of her regard for his Order, and a pledge of salvation to all those who wore it devoutly, and persisted in the practice of good works. So soon as this became public, the faithful crowded to receive the Scapular. Kings and Princes donned the Blessed Virgin's livery, in order to dedicate themselves to her service and

place themselves under her powerful protection. Nothing contributed so efficaciously to the spread of this devotion as the numerous graces conferred on those who wore the Scapular. Of the many miracles on record, we will cite one. At the siege of Montpellier, a soldier, who wore the Scapular, was hit by a ball while storming the town. The ball went right through all his garments until it reached the Scapular, when it glanced backwards and fell flattened to the ground, without his having sustained the slightest injury. Louis XIII., King of France, was present at the siege, and witnessed this event which impressed him so deeply that he too robed himself in this holy garb, the miraculous effects of which he had just witnessed.

Practice.

When the clock strikes, say one " Hail Mary ".

20th DAY.

The Dolours of Mary.

1st Part.

At the Presentation in the Temple, the sword of anguish pierced Mary's heart; she grieved for her Son, for herself, and for the human race.

1. WITH REGARD TO HER SON. The holy Simeon foretold that Jesus should be a rock of offence to the world, and a stumbling-stone to many. By these words Mary comprehended that her Son would be exposed to much opposition and persecution on the part of Jews, and heathens too. Simeon's words were ever in her mind. She kept them in her heart, constantly meditating on the sufferings her beloved Son was destined to endure. What bitterness for Mary. Is thy life, O reader, in harmony with that of thy Redeemer? Prove thy ways, and see in what to amend.

2. WITH REGARD TO MARY HERSELF. Of her, Simeon had said: "*And thy own heart a sword shall pierce*". From that instant the mere sight of Jesus,

who was destined to endure such inhuman treatment, was as a sharp sword piercing her inmost soul. *I gave my dearest child a tender kiss,* she tells St. Bridget, *and at once the kiss of Judas came to my mind; I nourished Him with milk from my Virgin breast, that reminded me of the gall and vinegar which He would drink on the Cross, and filled me with the deepest anguish.* O life-long, cruel martyrdom! Have compassion on her, and imitate her by constant meditation on thy Redeemer's sufferings.

3. WITH REGARD TO MANKIND. Simeon had told Mary that her Son should be a source of salvation to many, but also a stone of stumbling to others. Reflect, O my soul, how this announcement must have wounded our Blessed Lady's heart, that heart which glowed with an ardent desire for the salvation of sinners. What is Jesus to thee? A fount of salvation or a rock of offence? This depends on thee. Jesus will be thy salvation if thou earnestly desirest Him so to be.

PRAYER.

Tower of David, Tower of Ivory, pray for us!

O Blessed Virgin, thou art a tower of strength to all true disciples of Jesus thy beloved Son.

As David's tower, lofty and mighty, thou art the defence of the Holy City, the Church of thy Son. Lovely and spotless art thou; strong and mighty as a tower of ivory. Model of purity, mirror and example of every virtue, intercede for us, shield us from the temptations of the foe who aims at nothing less than robbing our hearts of their purity and hurling our souls to destruction. Be thou ever our strong tower against the enemy, so that we may win the victor's palm. Amen.

EXAMPLE.

St. Bernardine of Sienna.

The Saint whose Feast the Church celebrates on the 20th of May, was born in 1380; from youth upwards, his heart glowed with ardent love to the Blessed Mother of God, whose image he loved to contemplate with feelings of reverence and joy. It was his wont to pay a daily visit to a certain image, erected over one of the gates of Sienna, the sight of which inspired him with special feelings of devotion. This zeal on the pious youth's part was so well pleasing to the Mother of Mercy, that he was rewarded by a vocation to the monastic life. After entering the Order of St. Francis, and receiving many graces and favours from Mary, she

one day appeared to him, addressing him thus: "So well pleasing is thy devotion to me, that in addition to the great reward destined for thee, I endow thee with the gift of preaching, and power to work miracles. These are the gifts I have entreated from my Divine Son, in addition to which I promise thee that thou shalt hereafter participate in the eternal glory I enjoy in Heaven." The results proved the truth of these promises. St. Bernardine was a most zealous preacher of the Word; he irradiated the Church of God by the light of his doctrine, as well as by the splendour of his miracles, and sanctity of his life. What glorious fruits of devotion to Mary; and what blessed results of a lofty vocation (the gift of Mary), grace to follow which is bestowed on those who look to her for guidance! May preachers, teachers, and all who desire to advance their fellow-creatures' spiritual welfare, be constant in their devotion to Mary, and look to her for aid. Thus will they win more souls than by the study of many books, which, though they be marked by much oratorical beauty, are perhaps written in a spirit entirely foreign to the truth, and not in harmony with the wisdom of the Cross. A simple thought, inspired by God, and uttered under the inspiration of the Holy Ghost, can effect more good

than all the so-called morality, extracted from heterodox, or irreligious works. That which proceeds from God, leads to God. Eloquence and logic may win a man the name of orator, or scholar (and to strive to acquire a good style, is certainly a most praiseworthy endeavour); but only by Divine Grace, prayer, a pious life, and deep devotion to Mary, can one become an apostle, convert sinners, and be a faithful spiritual guide. Let us imitate St. Bernardine; then shall we, like him, have recourse to Mary for aid.

Practice.

Have a picture of the Blessed Virgin in your chamber, or carry one about your person, e.g., the medal of the Immaculate Conception.

21st DAY.

The Dolours of our Lady.

2nd Part.

Mary's grief at losing her Son; the origin, depth, and duration of this sorrow.

1. THE CAUSE OF MARY'S GRIEF. In losing Jesus, Mary lost her all; for Jesus was the origin and source of all her joy. What horror and alarm she must have felt on missing her beloved Son! What bitter tears she must have shed at failing to find Him among her kinsfolk and acquaintance!—When thou sinnest, thou, too, losest Jesus, thy Friend, thy Father, and thy God. After such a loss, canst thou enjoy peace of mind, laugh, and jest, as if nothing had occurred!

2. THE MAGNITUDE OF MARY'S GRIEF. What tormenting, disquieting thoughts must have torn Mary's heart, on being unable to find her Son. She could not imagine what had become of Him, where He was tarrying, nor for how long a time she should be deprived of His presence, nor even whether the moment might not have arrived when He was to fall into the hands of His foes. What

fearful uncertainty!—And how is it with thee when thou, by sin, hast lost, or thinkest thou hast lost, thy Saviour? Dost thou do thy utmost to find Him again?

3. THE DURATION OF MARY'S GRIEF. For three days and three nights the mournful Mother was deprived of her beloved Son. "Where art Thou," she exclaimed, sighing and weeping. "Where art Thou, my Jesus! my beloved Son? How long wilt Thou absent Thyself from me? Return, my Love, to Thy bereaved Mother. When Thou art present, all bitterness is sweet, without Thee, life is more bitter than death." In spite of her intense grief and longing, Jesus hid Himself for three days. Dost thou know the reason why He left His Mother mourning so long? Doubtless, the more richly to reward her patience. For this reason Jesus so often permits thee to suffer pain and anguish. When this is the case, think of Jesus, hie thee to Him; think of Mary, and humble thyself beneath the Mighty Hand of God. So shalt thou find consolation and win much merit.

PRAYER.

House of Gold, pray for us!

Most blessed Virgin, Chosen of God to be the

Mother of Him who is our Redeemer and the source of all our joy. Truly wert thou that House of Gold which the Eternal Father had prepared as a dwelling for His Son. For nine months the Creator of Heaven and Earth abode within thy Virgin-womb, therefore it behoved that House to be costly, unique, and precious, because of the pure, ardent, and strong love, which animated the Virgin-breast of her who was indeed blessed among women! Thou hast found favour with God; intercede for us that we too may find favour in His Sight, grow in love to Jesus, remain faithful unto death, so that we may be worthy of His indwelling Presence, and hereafter possess Him through all Eternity. Amen.

EXAMPLE.

St. Andrew Corsini.

The early life of this Saint teaches us the alacrity with which sinners should correspond with the call of Divine Grace. Before Andrew saw the light, his parents solemnly dedicated him to the Blessed Virgin, as the first-fruit of their union. The night preceding his birth, his mother Peregrina had an alarming dream. She dreamt that she had given birth to a wolf, which ran into

a Church, and was there transformed into a lamb. This was a type of Andrew himself. His pious parents spared no pains to give him a good and Christian education; but evil associates, love of play, and wordly pleasures seduced him from virtue's paths. He grew from bad to worse; was lacking in affection and obedience to his parents, and was a source of much anxiety to his friends. Meanwhile, his mother, remembering her dream, ceased not to intercede with Mary on his behalf. One day that Andrew was preparing to join a pleasure-party, he behaved in such an unbecoming manner to his mother that she burst into bitter tears, exclaiming in the intensity of her grief: "Verily, my son, thou art that wolf which I beheld in my dream". Surprised at these words, Andrew asked their meaning, whereupon Peregrina related her dream, and how she and her husband had dedicated their child to Mary, before his birth. This made such an impression on Andrew that he could not close his eyes that night. He ceased not to supplicate our Blessed Lady, saying: "Virgin-Mother, since I am thy servant, I will henceforth serve thee incessantly. I ask but one favour, that thou wilt obtain me the forgiveness of my sins." As soon as the day dawned, he repaired to the Carmelite Church, threw himself on his knees

before Mary's image, offered himself to the Mother of Divine Grace, as a wolf whose most ardent desire it was to be transformed into a lamb. He begged this so ardently and repeatedly that at last his prayer was heard. In order to serve the Blessed Virgin more perfectly, he requested admission into the Order; his request was granted, and his after-life verified the truth of his mother's dream. His example teaches us how powerful our Lady's intercession is when she supplicates for forgiveness and grace. Andrew made rapid advances in virtue, and soon became a model of perfection. At the commands of his superiors, he, later on, became a priest, and was afterwards elected Bishop; but in every relation of life he retained the warmest devotion for Mary, his mighty protectress, whose glory he strove to augment by every means in his power. At last, God called him hence to enter on eternal bliss. He died in the year 1373, and experienced, even in the hour of death, the blessed fruits of Mary's intercession.

PRACTICE.

Be diligent in reciting the Angelus.

22ND DAY.

OUR LADY'S DOLOURS.

3RD PART.

Mary's grief at the Crucifixion of her Son. This was a threefold grief; she mourned over her Son's physical sufferings, his anguish of heart and mind.

1. WITH REGARD TO OUR LORD'S PHYSICAL SUFFERINGS. Mary beheld the Body of her Son mangled and wounded from head to foot; His eyes suffused with tears; His countenance pale and disfigured; His members torn and bathed in blood; His Sacred Body extended on the Cross and transfixed by nails. Her heart shared each wound of Her Divine Son. As thou gazest on Jesus, mangled, torn, and nailed to the Cross for thy self-indulgence and thy want of mortification, well may the coldness of thy love cover thee with confusion!

2. HIS HEART-ANGUISH. Mary noted how the Heart of her Divine Son glowed with ardent love to man; she noted His magnanimous Sacrifice of

Himself upon the Altar of the Cross, in order to win forgiveness for the sinner. On the other hand, the compassionate Mother beheld the coldness and ingratitude with which this love would be repaid; she beheld the Priests, the Elders, and the very dregs of the populace, band together to deride Jesus and mock His sufferings; she beheld them give Him gall and vinegar to drink, and pierce His loving Heart. All this Mary saw, but with what feelings, and with what thoughts!

Mother of Sorrow—
> "Let me mingle tears with thee,
> Let me share with thee His pain
> Who for all my sins was slain,
> Who for me in torment died,"

that I may never more, by sin, crucify Him anew.

3. HIS PHYSICAL SUFFERINGS. Mary beheld the soul of Her beloved Jesus drowned in an ocean of grief and anguish unspeakable. In addition to all His other sufferings, He was also forsaken by His Heavenly Father. She knew those excruciating sorrows which racked His Soul, compared with which His Bodily Sufferings were as nought; she heard Him bewail His desolation; for three hours she watched Him in His Death Agony, unable to afford Him the slightest alleviation,

until at last He cried out with a loud voice: *Father, into Thy Hands I commend My Spirit;* and, bowing His Head, gave up the Ghost. Thus did a God-Incarnate lay down His life for man! Such were the sufferings endured by the Mother of that Divine Son! O miracle of Love! Jesus dies for love of us; and we, we live to torture and crucify Him afresh! Let us remember Calvary! Let us think of Jesus and Mary, and we shall never grieve them more.

Prayer.

Ark of the Covenant, pray for us!

Hail, Mother of Mercy, Queen of Heaven! Thou art our life, our sweetness, and our hope! Ark of the Covenant! more truly art thou entitled to that name than was the Ark prepared by Moses, in obedience to the Divine behest, as a type of the covenant between God and man. Within thy Virgin-womb, God became Incarnate; in thee dwelt Jesus, the Wisdom of the Father, the Author of the New Covenant; in thee was effected the reconcilation between God and man. Win us pardon for our past transgressions, and grace to serve Him faithfully for the time to come. And as the Ark of the Covenant was ever a place

of refuge to the Israelites in every time of trouble and danger, so be thou our refuge, help, and strong tower; pray for us sinners, now, and at the hour of our death. Amen.

EXAMPLE.

St. Francis of Assisi.

It is a subject of satisfaction to every Christian that the greatest Saints have emulated each other in their devotion and love to Christ's Blessed Mother. We will cite one instance; that of St. Francis, the great servant of God. This Saint, the wonder of his age and the ornament of the Church of God, first saw the light at Assisi in the year 1182. He was specially chosen of God to be the glory of His Church, and to show forth the abundance of His goodness to the children of men. We say nothing of the other favours so richly bestowed on him by the Divine Hand; we but allude to his fervent love and devotion to Mary. In the ardour of his zeal for God, Francis had undertaken the restoration of three Churches, greatly in need of reparation. One of these was a Church dedicated to the Mother of God, *St. Mary of the Angels*, or *Portiuncula*, as it was called. This Church was his favourite resort;

thither he repaired to honour Mary as the Queen of the Celestial Choirs. He was wont to pass entire days and nights within this edifice, imploring Mary (the Mother of the Eternal Word of the Father), to intercede for the salvation of sinners. Through this powerful Advocate he obtained that fulness of the Spirit of Christ, for which he is so remarkable. One night, when Francis, according to custom, was praying in this Church and commending his Order to our Blessed Lady's protection, Jesus appeared, in company with His Divine Mother, and surrounded by an Angelic Host. The Saint went on praying most earnestly, saying: "Most Holy Lord of Heaven and Redeemer of the world, my Sweet Love, and thou, Queen of Angels, what superabundance of goodness has prompted you to descend from Heaven into this poor little Chapel?" And Jesus replied: "I have come with My Mother in order to take possession of this spot, so dear in Our eyes, that We may hand it over to you and yours." Moreover, it was revealed to the Saint that Mary had received himself and his disciples under her maternal protection, which both augmented his love and devotion to our Lady and made him strive vigorously to render his sons participators of the same. That which most increased the

fervour of his devotion to Mary was the wondrous indulgence he obtained by her intercession, and which is known as the *Indulgence* of the *Portiuncula*. Of this we will give a brief account. Francis was filled with the deepest sorrow for the sad condition of sinners; he bewailed their blindness, and often besought God for their conversion and amendment. One night whilst praying to this effect, an Angel appeared, telling him to repair to the Church, where he would meet Jesus, with His Blessed Mother and a multitude of Angels. Full of joy he hastened thither, and after testifying his deep reverence, Jesus spake thus to him: "Francis, on account of the zeal manifested by thee and thine for the salvation of souls, thou art permitted to ask one favour in their behalf, and this for the glory of My Name". Amid all these wonders wherewith he was encompassed, Francis proffered this petition; "Most Holy Father, though but a poor sinner, I humbly entreat Thee that Thou wouldest graciously grant a plenary indulgence to all such who visit this Church after having confessed their sins to a Priest. And I entreat the Blessed Virgin, Thy Mother and the Advocate of the whole human race, to intercede for me and obtain me this favour." Immediately Mary turned to Jesus begging Him to accord this

grace; and Jesus replied: "Francis, thou askest a great favour; but thou shalt receive still greater tokens of My approval. I grant thee the favour thou askest of Me; but nevertheless I desire thee to go to My Vicegerent and request him to grant this indulgence." Francis obeyed; and in presence of the Cardinals, Honorius III., after due examination into the facts of the case, granted, or rather, we should say, confirmed the wondrous Indulgence which this man of God, through Mary's intercession, had received from Christ Himself. In all the events of his life he had recourse to Mary, his trust in whom was second only to that he placed in Jesus. Among other practices introduced in her honour, he instituted a fast of six weeks, preparatory to the Feast of the Assumption, rigorously observing the same. Among the many prayers addressed by him to Mary, we quote one:

Hail Mary, ever Virgin, Mother of God, Most Holy Queen, in whom dwells the fulness of grace. Peerless art thou among women, thou who art both Daughter and Handmaid of the Eternal Father, the Great King, Who chose thee to be the Mother of His Own Well-Beloved Son; also thou art the Spouse of the Holy Ghost, the Comforter. Hail thou Palace, Sanctuary, and Mother of our Lord Jesus Christ! I reverence all those virtues

with which thou art so replete. O mild and gracious one, intercede on our behalf with Jesus, thy beloved Son, conjuring Him by His Infinite Mercy, and in virtue of His Holy Incarnation and bitter Death, that He will pardon our sins. Amen.

PRACTICE.

Read some spiritual book daily, if only for one quarter of an hour.

23rd DAY.

The Joys of Mary.

1st Part.

The birth of Jesus filled Mary's heart with joy. She beheld in Him the world's Saviour, Teacher, and Exemplar.

1. THE SAVIOUR OF THE WORLD. Under this name He had been announced to the Shepherds. "*Unto you is born a Saviour.*" Mary well knew that her well-beloved Son had come to redeem mankind. What joy must have filled her heart on first beholding and embracing Jesus! O my soul, never forget that Jesus came into the world for the redemption of the whole human race, thyself among the rest; see that thou correspond with His loving designs.

2. THE WORLD'S TEACHER. The Prophet Isaiah had said: "*Thine eyes shall behold thy Teachers.*" Doubtless, this prophecy alluded chiefly to Mary. She had the supreme happiness of first beholding the World's Divine Teacher, Who would give humanity wholly new lessons respecting humility, poverty, and abnegation; in a word, Who would teach them the Lesson of the Cross.

What progress hast thou made in the School of this Divine Master? Hast thou learnt from Him humility, lowliness of heart, and self-denial?

3. THE WORLD'S EXEMPLAR. It was with the intensest joy and deepest astonishment that Mary beheld the method adopted by Her Divine Son. He taught by example rather than by precept. He would one day preach humility; but before doing this by word of mouth, He practised it by selecting a manger for His birth-place. He would hereafter teach His disciples to practise self-denial and mortification; He set them the example, choosing a stall for His abode, and this in the severity of Winter. He came to teach us poverty of spirit and patience under trial; here we behold Him bereft of all the conveniences of life, having nought save a little hay or straw, and a poor swaddling robe.

Thou findest it hard to comply with the Evangelical Precepts; contemplate this Divine Mother, and all thy difficulties will vanish!

PRAYER.

Gate of Heaven, pray for us!

O Most Blessed Virgin! Eve, by her disobedience, closed Heaven's portals; by thy obe-

dience thou hast reopened them. By thee, the Divine Son, the World's Redeemer, came down from Heaven to Earth; through thee, the grace of God has been revealed to us in Jesus; through thee our prayers ascend to Heaven, and through thee the faithful servants of the Lord enter the haven of eternal bliss. Verily thou art the Gate of Heaven, by which we have access to our Heavenly home. Pray for us sinners! Of ourselves we are unworthy to enter Heaven; by our many sins we have merited Hell; but thou art our help and succour. Win us grace to amend our lives and persevere to the end in the practice of good works, so that, through thee, we may hereafter enter the Eternal Kingdom. Amen.

EXAMPLE.

St. Ignatius of Loyola.

As it is by Mary that we have received Jesus, there is no better way of approaching Jesus, than by Mary. The life of St. Ignatius of Loyola is a striking proof of the truth of this assertion. This Saint, elected by Providence to be the founder of the Society of Jesus, and to be the instrument of much good to God's Church during troublous times, attributed his conversion, and the many

graces he received, principally to the Blessed Virgin's intercession. After being wounded at the Siege of Pampeluna, which town he had so heroically defended, he resolved to consecrate himself wholly to the Service of God. He commenced by dedicating himself to the Service of Mary, earnestly entreating her to present him to her Beloved Son, and intercede with Him on his behalf. One night, when kneeling in prayer before our Lady's image, entreating her with tears that she would graciously accept him, the Blessed Virgin appeared in company with her Divine Son; and the most wondrous results ensued as regarded Ignatius. His heart was wholly transformed; and he who hitherto had been so often tormented by disquieting thoughts was thenceforth and for ever wholly liberated from their thraldom. A man of such magnanimous temper as Ignatius, was not content to do things by halves. When recovered from the effects of his wounds, he quitted the paternal roof, in order to withdraw wholly from the world and give himself up entirely to the service of Jesus Christ.

He repaired to Montserat, a Benedictine Monastery, greatly renowned in Spain because of its miraculous image of the Blessed Virgin, which was an object of much devotion. As he journeyed

thither, he reflected as to what offering would be most acceptable to Mary, and took upon himself the vow of perpetual chastity. On reaching the Church, he made a general confession, weeping bitterly, and having, in accordance with the practice of chivalry, spent a whole night weeping and praying before our Lady's image, hung his sword upon her altar as a token that he intended henceforth to serve none but Mary and her Divine Son. Later on, Ignatius was called on to found the new order of the Society of Jesus; but from respect and devotion to our Lady, without whose aid he would commence no undertaking, the Feast of the Assumption was selected for this purpose. On that day, he and his companions assembled at Montmartre, near Paris, where they took their vows, renewing them annually on the same day. He always wore our Lady's image on his breast; composed many prayers in her honour, and ever had recourse to her for counsel and aid. He strove to inspire his companions with tender love to our Blessed Lady, that she might reward them by her constant protection, and aid them in fulfilling the arduous duties of their vocation. One day, when his relation, Father Araoz, sorrowfully took leave of him, Ignatius, to console him, gave him the image of our Lady which he

had been so long accustomed to wear suspended round his neck, assuring him that she had never failed to aid him in vanquishing all temptations hostile to purity; and, indeed, we learn from his own pen, that Mary frequently appeared to him, that she aided him in a special manner in compiling his celebrated work, *The Spiritual Exercises*, as well as in drawing up the Constitutions of the Society of Jesus, and that throughout the varied course of his life she ever aided him with true maternal love. Happy they who honour Mary, and trust in her with filial affection!

PRACTICE.

Do not neglect to recite the Rosary, attentively meditating its several mysteries.

24th Day.

The Joys of Mary.

2nd Part.

Her joy at the Resurrection was a threefold joy; she rejoiced to see her Son again, she rejoiced to behold the Apostles once more, and she rejoiced at the thought of the future resurrection of the faithful.

1. HER JOY AT RE-BEHOLDING HER SON. The sad and mournful Mother had followed Jesus to Golgotha, bathing His footprints with her tears. What joy and happiness unspeakable must have been her's on beholding her Beloved Son, His sufferings and humiliations ended, now radiant in Celestial Glory! What mutual congratulations they must have exchanged! And thus will it ever be! They who share Christ's sufferings, will also participate in His glory and exaltation.

2. HER JOY ON AGAIN BEHOLDING THE APOSTLES. By the death of their Divine Lord and Master, the Apostles were left forsaken, and scattered hither

and thither. Sorrowful, dejected, and disconsolate, they wandered as sheep without a shepherd. On the third day, Jesus arose triumphantly, and Mary had the inexpressible delight to see the Apostles re-assembling around their Divine Lord. By thy repeated desertion of Jesus, thou hast often grieved thy Celestial Mother's heart! Rejoice her now by thy speedy return and constant fidelity to Him for the future.

3. HER JOY AT THE RESURRECTION OF THE FAITHFUL. Mary saw her Beloved Son arisen from the dead, and girt with immortality; this was to her a guarantee of the resurrection of the faithful. She had indeed already seen some of the fruits of His Resurrection in the persons of those elect saints who had already risen from their graves, with Jesus, and in virtue of His merits. Belief in the future Resurrection of the Dead is the surest basis of a truly Christian life; if we are indeed true members of Christ, we shall also share the glory of our Head. If the Head has arisen, the members will do so too. See then that, with God's help, thou arise now from the death of sin to a new, holy life, that hereafter thou mayest arise to Eternal Life, and spend a blissful Eternity in the presence of thy Lord.

Prayer.

Morning Star, pray for us!

Most Blessed Virgin-Mother, thou art the morning star who hast heralded in Jesus the Sun of Righteousness, the world's true light. Thy appearance on earth was the dawn of that day so full of happiness to all the sons of earth. By thy light, thou hast scattered all the shades of sin and darkness. Thou illuminest our hearts, teaching us to know Jesus, in whom dwelleth the fulness of light, truth, and grace. Happy they, who have thee for their guide! Thou wilt not fail to lead them to Jesus. O gracious Virgin, be thou our light, so that we may shun the works of darkness and tread the path that leads to Jesus the Eternal Light, and, with thee, gaze on Him and praise Him throughout Eternity. Amen.

Example.

St. Gregory.—Sta. Maria Maggiore.'

During the pontificate of St. Gregory the Great, the inhabitants of Rome experienced a fresh proof of Mary's special protection. At that epoch, a fearful plague ravaged most of the countries in

Europe, and Rome in particular. It was terrible to see the havoc it made; thousands were carried off by this fearful scourge, and that so suddenly as to leave the poor victims neither time nor opportunity to prepare for death. The Holy Father had already exhorted the people to repentance; special prayers had been enjoined and many vows made; but the evil seemed to augment rather than diminish. The alarm and misery of the inhabitants had attained their climax, when Gregory determined to have recourse again to Mary, and place himself wholly under her protection. He commanded that the miraculous portrait of the Blessed Virgin (attributed to St. Luke's pencil) should be taken from its wonted resting place, the Church of Sta. Maria Maggiore, and carried in procession through the city, priests and people taking part in the ceremony. The procession repaired to the beforementioned Basilica, the picture was carried in solemn pomp through the streets, and the result at once proved how effectual Mary's intercession is, if *with our whole heart* we invoke her aid and trust in her powerful protection. The plague was instantly arrested. Wherever the procession passed, the fell malady suddenly took its flight; and as it was passing Hadrian's Tomb (the Castle of St. Angelo), the Holy Father beheld an

Angel, in human form, sheathing a blood-stained sword, to testify that, in virtue of Mary's intercession, the scourge had been withdrawn. At the same time Angel-voices were heard saying: Regina cœli, lætare, Alleluia (Rejoice, O Queen of Heaven, Alleluia). The holy Pontiff added these words: "pray for us, Alleluia," and since that time the Church has enjoined this prayer to be recited at Easter-tide, when the Angelus sounds.

Not long ago, when cholera threatened the whole of Europe, and all means to arrest the evil appeared unavailing, Gregory XVI., following the example of his saintly predecessors, commanded that sermons should be preached in every Church, exhorting the people to repentance; he appointed days of fasting and humiliation, enjoined certain public devotions, and finally resolved that our Blessed Lady's picture should be escorted in solemn procession from the Church of Sta. Maria Maggiore to St. Peter's, there to remain exposed to the veneration of the faithful. This took place on the 8th September, 1835. Towards sunset the picture was deposited in the *New Church of the Oratorians (Maria in Vallicella)*, where it remained exposed for veneration until September 15th. Then, accompanied by the Holy Father, the Sacred College of Cardinals, the Roman

Clergy, and an innumerable crowd of the faithful, it was transported to St. Peter's, where it remained on the Papal Altar, above St. Peter's tomb, until the 24th of September. On that day it was borne in solemn pomp to the Church of the Jesuit novitiate, called the "Gesu," where it remained till the 30th of September, when the Holy Father, several Cardinals, and the Roman Clergy, re-escorted it, with prayers and hymns, to its wonted resting place, where it had been left undisturbed since the pontificate of St. Gregory, that is, since the above recorded event, which took place in the year 590.

We are sure the following prayer, engraved on metal at the back of the miraculous picture, will be acceptable to every devout client of Mary:

Hail, thou most sublime Queen of Peace, most Holy Mother of God! By the Sacred Heart of Jesus, thy Son, the Prince of Peace, appease the Divine Anger, and give us peace. Remember, O most gracious Virgin Mary, that never was it known that any one who sought thy intercession was left unaided. Mother of the Word Incarnate, despise not my petitions, but in thy mercy hear and answer them, O clement, O pious, O sweet Virgin Mary. Amen.

Practice.

Take pleasure in narrating such things as may contribute to Mary's honour and inspire confidence in her.

25TH DAY.

THE JOYS OF MARY.

3RD PART.

Mary's joy at her Son's Ascension: she rejoiced because of he place whither He ascended; she rejoiced because of those who accompanied Him thither; and she rejoiced in the consequences of His Ascension.

1. THE PLACE WHITHER HE ASCENDED. Jesus ascended to Heaven to take possession of His Eternal Kingdom. He entered His Father's house, the goal of His pilgrimage, the home of rest after His many labours and trials, the crown and recompense of all His past sorrows. This thought filled the Blessed Virgin's heart with the sweetest joy. Do thou also often raise thy thoughts to Heaven, and earth's burdens will be the lighter to bear. Heaven is thy home; thither must thy longings tend; and by the practice of works of love and virtuous deeds must thou strive to advance daily nearer home.

2. HIS COMPANIONS. Mary beheld Jesus ascend to Heaven, surrounded by an innumerable band

of Holy Souls, who till now had been tarrying in Hades, awaiting the moment of their redemption. Take this well to heart; Jesus ascends to Heaven; but not alone : a countless host of the elect are with Him. Thou thinkest only of thyself; thou considerest it enough to ensure thy own salvation. . . . . But in this thou art greatly mistaken. *Thou shalt love thy neighbour as thyself.* Therefore do thy utmost to win many souls to God, and so add to the denizens of Heaven. Thus wilt thou multiply the fruits of thy Lord's Passion, rejoice His loving heart, and increase thy own merits.

3. WHY DID JESUS ASCEND TO HEAVEN ? After accomplishing the work of Redemption, Jesus ascended to Heaven, in order to prepare a place for His followers, to erect a throne for His Blessed Mother, and exalt her far above the Angelic host. How intensely Mary must have yearned to follow her Son, and abide with Him for ever! And we, unhappy children of earth, are so engrossed with transitory things as almost wholly to forget our Heavenly home, and the countless treasures which await us there. It is high time to pursue nobler aims; to despise the evanescent pleasures and deceitful charms of earth, and seek those things which are eternal. Our place is already prepared; let us strive to be worthy of it.

Prayer.

Health of the sick, pray for us.

In every malady of soul and body thou art our refuge, our help, most blessed Mother of God! By thy intercession thou hast healed countless numbers of the sick. Confiding in thy power and goodness, we too have recourse to thee. Heal our maladies, and give us health of soul and body, so that we may the better serve thee and thy Divine Son. Thou never failest to aid and console the sick, thou assuagest their pains, thou askest health for them, if it be for their spiritual good; thou aidest them in their last moments, and grantest them a happy death. Aid us too, dear Mother! Pray for us that we may be delivered from all our sufferings, or have patience and resignation to comply with the Divine Will, so that all our pains and trials may be sanctified to us. Amen.

Example.

St. Philip Neri.

The Church commemorates this Saint on the 26th of May. He was one of the greatest ornaments of the Church of God in the sixteenth century, and by his unwearied zeal in advancing the cause of Christianity, especially in the Eternal City, has

been rightly termed the Apostle of Rome. He was an elect vessel, chosen by God to glorify His name in the world, to stem the tide of vice, and advance the cause of virtue. From his childhood he gave signs of unusual perfection, which augmented with advancing years. His love and devotion to our Blessed Lady were deep and fervent in the extreme. Mary was the object of his heart's most ardent affection; her name was almost always on his lips, and to promote her honour and spread her praise abroad was his unwearying and constant aim. No child ever loved its earthly mother as tenderly as Philip loved Mary. He called her his love, his joy, his consolation, and uttered these words with such deep feeling and unction as frequently to move his hearers to tears. At times he passed entire nights in prayer, and held such reverent, loving, heartfelt converse with her, as if she were visibly present. And indeed, this kind mother did at times manifest herself to him, consoling him, gladdening his heart, and enriching him with many a grace. Such was the case during his old age, when laid upon a bed of sickness from which his physicians hardly thought he would ever rise again. Suddenly the saintly man was heard exclaiming: "O my most holy Mother, most amiable,

most beauteous, and blessed Mother!" The physicians and the priests present hastened to his side, and beheld him raised in the air, more than a foot above his bed, his arms outstretched as if he wished to clasp some one in their embrace, and the bystanders heard him (beside himself with joy) exclaim: "Dearest Lady, I am not worthy of this favour; I do not deserve that thou shouldst come to visit and heal me! What return shall I make thee if thou restorest me to health, I who have never done aught that is good?" .... The spectators were filled with surprise; some wept for joy; others trembled with alarm; and on one of the physicians asking him what he wanted, Philip lay down again on his bed, replying: "Did you not see the most Blessed Virgin who came to free me from my pain?" Whilst he thus spoke he appeared to recover consciousness, and on observing that there were several persons in the room, he hid his face and began to weep. The physicians, fearful lest this should do him harm, begged him to compose himself, and asked to feel his pulse; he replied: "I no longer need your assistance, the Blessed Virgin has been here and healed me". And indeed they found him perfectly restored, so that he rose next morning and pursued his usual avocations without experiencing the least inconvenience.

The Saint never wearied of exhorting all who approached him, to trust in our Blessed Lady, saying: "Believe me, my children, the surest way of obtaining any favour from God is to ask it of the Blessed Virgin; therefore say frequently: '*Virgin Mary, Mother of God, pray to Jesus for me*'". Our Lady not only restored St. Philip, but did the same for others, at his request. Cæsar Baronius, an intimate friend of the Saint, lay dangerously ill, the physicians tried every remedy, but all in vain. As the sick man felt himself near death, he dreamt he saw Philip fervently supplicating our Lord, repeating with child-like simplicity: "*Lord, spare my Cæsar, preserve my Cæsar; Thou must restore him to me!*" Thus he went on for some time, but to no avail. Then he addressed himself to the Blessed Virgin, entreating her to obtain this favour from her Son. And Mary heard his prayer; she turned to Jesus, begging that Baronius might recover, and he was instantly cured. On another occasion Mary aided our Saint in an equally wondrous manner. They were building a new church, when, early one day, St. Philip sent in all haste to the builder, bidding him at once remove the roof from a certain old building, which would certainly have fallen in during the night had not the Blessed Virgin

supported it with her own hands. On examining the building, it was found that the beams had moved from their position, so that the roof was left wholly unsupported. Philip took a special delight in visiting the wonder-working picture of Santa Maria Maggiore, and fervently exhorted his disciples to love and honour Mary; he also enjoined that in every Church or Oratory built by his children, there should be a picture of our Lady over each Altar. Through her intercession he won special graces for many, exhorting them to use the following little prayer: "Virgin Mary, Mother of God, pray to thy Jesus for me": sometimes he added: "Pray to thy Son Jesus for me, a sinner". Sometimes he enjoined these two words only: "Virgin and Mother!"—saying that so comprehensive were these words that they denoted Mary's full glory and sublimity, hence their efficacy to obtain from her every grace. Did we but love and trust Mary as St. Philip Neri did, how many a grace should we not receive from that tender Mother!

PRACTICE.

Pause, and reflect what good deed will be most pleasing to Mary; then carry it into effect this very day, for love of her.

26TH DAY.

MARY'S LIFE.

1ST PART.

The character of Mary's thoughts. They were holy and perfect; they ever dwelt on Him who, for our sake, became man; on Him who lies concealed beneath the Sacramental Veils, and who died on the Cross for us.

1. THE MYSTERY OF THE INCARNATION. She loved to dwell on this mystery, the thought of which filled her with wonder and admiration. As we are wont to think constantly on that which we hold most dear, so was it with Mary; she delighted to ponder this mystery; the more so, inasmuch as she had been chosen by the Blessed Trinity to be the Mother of the Eternal Word. May we too ever love to meditate on, and fathom the deep signification of those words: *The word was made flesh and dwelt amongst us!*

2. SHE THOUGHT OF HIM WHO LIES CONCEALED BENEATH THE EUCHARISTIC VEILS. Tradition tells us that Mary received Holy Communion daily, and some traditions even assert that in her case

the sacramental species remained unchanged from one Communion to the other. With what deep reverence and fervent love she must have adored Him who lay hidden beneath the Eucharistic veils, what glowing ardour must have filled her breast as she received into her heart Him whom she had conceived by the power of the Holy Ghost, and brought into the world for our salvation! If transports of ecstatic joy have filled the hearts of other Saints on receiving their hidden Lord, words must fail to describe Mary's deep emotions! In Holy Communion thou too receivest thy Divine Lord. How hast thou prepared thyself to welcome Him? How entertained that Divine Guest? Examine thyself and see what is lacking on thy part, so that thou mayest amend thy ways, and profit by the visit of that Heavenly Guest!

3. SHE THOUGHT OF HIM WHO WAS CRUCIFIED FOR US. Mary stood by the Cross of her Beloved Son; she beheld and shared all His pain and anguish. So deeply were these mournful mysteries imprinted on her maternal heart, that she never forgot them for a single instant. They were ever in her thoughts. So should it be with thee; make the sufferings of Jesus the constant subject of thy meditations, so wilt thou find grace to

vanquish thy spiritual foes and advance in the paths of virtue.

Prayer.

Refuge of Sinners, pray for us.

O Mother of Mercy, who rejectest none who flee to thee for aid. The vilest sinner finds a friend in thee, if he approach thee with lowly, humble, and contrite heart. Thou intercedest for him with Jesus, thy Divine Son, our Lord and Judge; thou shieldest him from the arm of His righteous judgment; thou defendest him from the attacks of his spiritual foe; thou dissipatest the cloud of unbelief and doubt, filling his heart with the sweet balm of hope. How many souls thou hast snatched from Hell! In how many hearts thou hast awakened contrition and an earnest resolve to amend their lives! Have pity on us also! To thee do we sigh, to thee do we cry, poor banished children of Eve. Obtain for us truly penitent hearts, and grace to avoid all sin for the time to come. Reconcile us to thy Son now, and intercede for us at our last hour. Amen.

Example.

St. Mary of Egypt.

Such as have been so unhappy as to lead a

sinful life, can do nought better than flee to Mary with truly penitent hearts, that by her intercession they may obtain forgiveness of their sins. Thus did St. Mary of Egypt. She was a native of Egypt, and from the date of her conversion led a most penitential life. She narrated the details of her life to the Abbot Zosimus, on meeting him in the desert one day. We extract the following from the writings of St. Sophronius, Patriarch of Jerusalem:

At the age of twelve, Mary, despite her parent's opposition, repaired to Alexandria, where for many years she led a most sinful life. One day, in Summer-time, she noticed a number of persons starting for Jerusalem in order to celebrate the Feast of the Exaltation of the Cross; she embarked also, and continued her sinful course, even on the journey. As the people were proceeding to the Church where the Holy Cross was exposed to the veneration of the faithful, Mary joined them. On attempting to enter the Church, she felt held back as if by an invisible hand. This occurred three or four times. Deeply impressed by this, and feeling convinced that her sinfulness was the cause of her being so repulsed, she began to weep bitterly. Whilst tarrying at the porch of the Church, sighing, mourning, and striking her breast in a spirit of

contrition, a picture of the Divine Mother, painted on the wall, suddenly struck her eye. This sight inspired her with courage, and she turned to the Queen of Heaven with these words: "Holy Virgin, Mother of God, I know that the sins with which my life is stained render me unworthy of thy notice. Thou art a spotless Virgin; so holy and pure, that the sight of a soul so sin-stained as mine must fill thee with abhorrence. Yet I have heard that the Saviour whom thou hadst the happiness to bear, came into the world to call sinners to repentance. I entreat thee to have pity on me, and permit me to enter the Church, unworthy though I am, that I may not be deprived of the happiness of beholding that precious wood which was bathed in the Blood of thy Son. In the name of that same Redeemer, I promise thee to desist from my evil ways; and so soon as I have venerated the holy Cross, I will renounce the world, and follow whither thou leadest me, O Holy Virgin, my Advocate, and my Guide!"

Her prayer ended, she felt herself full of confidence; and on again essaying to enter the Church, experienced not the slightest opposition. She went in, joined the rest of the congregation in adoring the Cross; then, weeping bitterly, pro-

strated herself to kiss the ground of those holy places, deeply moved by the mercy of God and His readiness to welcome the returning sinner; her devotion ended, she returned to our Lady's image, and, kneeling down before it, thanked her for her gracious aid, earnestly entreating her to point out the course of life she should pursue, in order best to atone for the past. Whilst thus pouring out her heart, she heard a voice, as if in the distance, calling to her and saying: "If thou crossest Jordan, thou wilt find rest". She arose instantly, and fixing her gaze on the picture, exclaimed, weeping: "Virgin of Virgins! Thou channel of grace and salvation, forsake me not, I most humbly entreat thee!" She then hastily crossed Jordan, and buried herself in the depths of the wilderness. There she lived for more than forty years, leading a most penitential life. She was frequently assailed by violent temptations, but overcame them all by Mary's aid. "In all my struggles (thus she expressed herself to Abbot Zosimus), I raised my heart to the Virgin Immaculate who had received me so graciously; I begged her never to forsake me in my desert home; and she never has forsaken me, but has been my constant guide, and has aided me in all my difficulties." And at the close of life, by Mary's intercession, this holy penitent

had the extreme happiness of receiving the last Sacraments, at the hands of Abbot Zosimus, and of being reconciled to, and united with her Divine Lord for ever! Happy the sinner who flees to Mary for succour, guidance, and grace to amend his life. Not only will he find grace with God; but he is on the road to sanctity.

Practice.

Encourage others to venerate the Divine Mother, and by your own conduct atone for the insults offered to her and to her Divine Son.

27TH DAY.

MARY'S LIFE.

2ND PART.

The topic of Mary's conversation.—She spoke of God, for God, and with God.

1. SHE SPOKE OF GOD. Out of the fulness of the heart, the mouth speaketh. Closely united to God, and loving Him with so ardent a love, what could form the topic on which Mary conversed with the early Christians, save that of God? Her words were words of glowing love, which sank deep into her hearers' hearts, inflaming their ardent affection to her Divine Lord. Is not thy silence regarding God a proof of the weakness of thy love? And yet, frequent converse on God and divine things is a potent means of cherishing and augmenting our love to our Creator.

2. SHE SPOKE FOR GOD. There is no doubt that the Blessed Virgin, that tender Mother of the faithful, observed the duties of hospitality; that she not only welcomed persons to her hearth, but

that she visited them also, in order to console, instruct, and cheer them. But this, only when God's honour required this loving service at her hands. Then, with what caution she weighed her words, she, whose every heart-pulse beat with love to God! Though thou canst not make God the constant theme of thy discourse (for not only might the thoughtless votaries of the world find such conversation distasteful, but it might also prove a stone of stumbling, and rock of offence to them), do thou, at least, speak for God; *i.e.*, in conversation, let your aim be to please God, and promote His honour and glory.

3. SHE SPOKE WITH GOD. Mary conversed far more with God, than of, or for God. Her whole life was one of continual prayer and contemplation; even during her hours of brief repose, her heart was still united to God, and full of love for Him. What a blessed privilege thus to commence the eternal union here below! but it reminds us how deep is our wretchedness and imperfection. Let us lay our hand upon our breast, and, with heart-felt sincerity, confess how little time we devote to prayer, and how imperfect our supplications are. We find no leisure to converse with God; and yet we squander whole hours, perhaps days also, in idleness. Prayer seems irksome, so cold are our

hearts! And yet prayer should be our most congenial occupation, our school, our light, our comfort, our strength, and the life of our existence. Lord, teach us how to pray; Mother of Jesus, win us this grace! We are rich enough, if we know how to pray aright; for he who does this, receives the thing for which he prays.

Prayer.

Comforter of the afflicted, help of Christians, pray for us!

Most loving Mother! no suppliant ever had recourse to thee in vain. Whatever our needs, thy ear is ever open to our cry. Thou art the comforter of the afflicted; thou driest the exile's tears. Thou art the help of Christians. As the Mother of Christ, thou viewest thyself as their Mother and Advocate. O good and powerful Mother! Come to our aid, and deliver us from all our troubles. Succour the Christian flock, so hard beset on every side; protect the faithful, especially such as are in danger of losing their faith, that pearl of great price; succour the Church, that her foes may not prevail against her; humble her opponents and persecutors; exalt those who invoke thy name, and place their trust in thee. Show

thyself our Mother. Intercede for each one of us, that we may lead a Christian life, and hereafter reign with Christ throughout Eternity. Amen.

EXAMPLE.

St. Mary Magdalen of Pazzi.

The Church commemorates this Virgin Saint on the 27th of May; therefore we select her for our contemplations to-day, on account of her marked devotion to our blessed Lady. Wonderful is God in all His Saints, so says the Royal Prophet, but most wondrously were His love, omnipotence, and wisdom manifested in this Saintly Virgin. Even in childhood, God endowed her with many signal graces, which she repaid with such ardent love, and such fervent zeal in His Service, that she was more like an Angel than a mortal. It was most touching to note the extreme diligence with which she watched over the purity of her heart, and her anxiety to render true and faithful service to her Divine Master. Jesus and Mary were the chosen objects of her love. Her eyes were ever fixed on the latter, that through her she might find grace with Jesus, and also that she might learn how to please Him; she strove to imitate Mary's virtues, in order that she might be the more acceptable to

Jesus; and when meditating on the mysteries of Redemption, on our Lord's earthly life, or Heavenly Glory, she accustomed herself to dwell on the share Mary had in all these mysteries, and her zealous co-operation in their accomplishment. Hence her heart glowed with love, not only to Jesus, but also to the Divine Mother who had given birth to the world's Redeemer. Mary Magdalen of Pazzi entered the Carmelite Order in Florence. From that moment she strove, with redoubled energy, to promote the glory of God and that of the Virgin Mother. Mary frequently manifested herself to our Saint, in order to cheer and encourage her. And to strengthen her in virtue, God permitted her to endure manifold and heavy temptations; but however fierce the struggle, Mary never failed to aid her in overcoming the attacks of her spiritual foe. She commended all her companions to the protection of the Blessed Virgin, who on one occasion revealed to her with what maternal care she watches over all those who flee to her for aid. Her love to Mary evinced itself in a most marked manner, on the days set apart in our Lady's honour. How carefully she prepared herself to celebrate them, how earnestly she looked forward to their arrival! For her they were feasts indeed. The mystery of the day

wholly engrossed her mind; and so acceptable to God was this zeal, that she was rewarded with a keen insight as to Mary's glory and exaltation. These supernatural graces greatly contributed to augment her love and devotion to our Blessed Lady. Mary Magdalen had also a most fervent love for the Cross; her most ardent desire being to suffer with Jesus, and by suffering to be transformed into His image: hence her favourite saying: "Live and suffer". Whilst the majority of persons shun the Cross, and even the best among them yearn for some alleviation to their sufferings, and long to be freed from them, this was not the case with our Saint; so dear to her was the Cross, that, although in other respects life had no attraction for her, she entreated God to prolong her days, in order that she might be able to suffer more for Jesus. The remembrance of the pangs endured by the Mother of Sorrows as she stood by the Cross of her dying Son, inspired Mary Magdalen of Pazzi with an ardent love for suffering. God granted this heroic Virgin's prayer. She endured the most acute bodily pains, and this (in accordance with her own express wish) without any sensible spiritual consolation, such as God is wont to grant His servants in their last hour. Magdalen endured this patiently and joyfully, and,

full of suffering, departed this life in the year 1607, with heart-felt trust in Mary. May we too strive to honour our Blessed Lady, by imitating her virtues! And, especially in time of suffering, may we follow her example, stand with her beneath the Cross, and bewail our Saviour's sufferings, and our own sins! Then shall we indeed experience that Mary is the Mother of Mercy; the Comforter of the Afflicted; and the Help of all true disciples of Christ.

PRACTICE.

Never pass our Lady's image without paying her some mark of respect; and, when possible, recite a " Hail, Mary".

28TH DAY

MARY'S LIFE.

3RD PART.

How did Mary spend her time? Hers was a life of action, contemplation, and the two combined.

1. HER LIFE OF ACTION. By this, we here mean promoting her neighbours' welfare. After her Divine Son's Death and Ascension, as Mother of the faithful, Mary was ever unwearied in promoting the welfare of her Son's disciples; she comforted and cheered them; instructed and strengthened them in the Faith, of which, say the holy Fathers, she was the first and most distinguished teacher. And thou, O reader, in what dost thou contribute to thy neighbours' welfare? Remember that both thy soul and his are ransomed by the precious Blood of Christ!

2. IN CONTEMPLATION. By a contemplative life, we mean a life spent in meditating on Heavenly things. Who can tell in what perfection Mary must have possessed the faculty of contemplation? No

mortal loved the things of Heaven as Mary loved them, or ever had such a keen insight into them! —In proportion to thy ability, do thou also contemplate the mysteries of the Faith, and turn them to thy own spiritual profit; frequently raise thy heart to God, in fervent prayers and pious ejaculations; think of Him often when you are at work; consecrate all your actions to Him, and He will bless your labour, and rich will be your reward!

3. THE TWO COMBINED. The sacred bond of charity unites contemplation with works of active beneficence. So was it with Mary; in fulfilling her spiritual duties she never lost sight of her neighbour's welfare; and while labouring actively on his behalf, her heart was ever raised to God, love to Whom prompted her every act of charity to those around her. She divided her time between prayer and works of love!—Blessed occupation! Never do we leave God's Presence to better purpose than when we do so in order to render loving service to our neighbour; and never does God welcome us so readily as when we have been serving Him in the person of our neighbours. Meditate on the manner in which Mary passed her time; but, above all, see that you imitate her example, as far as in you lies.

Prayer.

Queen of Angels, pray for us!

O star-crowned Mother! thou surpassest the most exalted Angels, in merits, grace, and sanctity. The celestial spirits bow before thee. They honour and praise thee as the first of all created beings, as the most favoured of God's creatures and as the most blessed of women, inasmuch as thou wert found worthy to be the Mother of Him Who is the Source of Life. Glory and honour be to thee! Thy throne is in the highest Heavens. Be thou our gracious Queen, and loving Mother; we praise thee in concert with the Angelic Choirs, and place ourselves beneath thy protection. From the throne of thy glory, cast a gracious eye on us, who are encircled with so many dangers and trials; pray to thy Son Jesus for us, that we may emulate the purity of the Angels, so that we too may one day enjoy the Beatific Vision, and praise our Creator throughout Eternity. Amen.

Example.

St. Aloysius.

If the pure of heart are specially dear to the

Blessed Virgin, how dear must St. Aloysius be, whom, on account of his purity, the Church styles *an angelic youth*. Historians tell us that he owed his life to Mary's intercession. So critical was his mother's condition, that the medical attendants despaired of the child's life. On hearing that, humanly speaking, there was no hope, she turned to Mary with increased confidence, vowing that, if all went well with her, she would make a pilgrimage to Loretto, with her child. Hardly had she done this, when, contrary to all expectation, she was happily delivered. Aloysius never forgot this favour; he considered himself as Mary's servant, seeing that to her he was indebted for his very existence. With what reverence his infantine lips pronounced the names of Jesus and Mary! How devoutly he recited the prayers his mother taught him! At the age of seven, he had certain hours set apart for prayer; he was wont to say the Angelus, and other prayers, in Mary's honour. When nine years old, he was sent to Florence to prosecute his studies, in which he made rapid progress, and not only in them, but in the spiritual life also; his devotion to Mary became so fervent, that at the very sound of her name his heart glowed with love. The fervour of these sentiments was considerably augmented by the perusal of a little

book, having the *Mysteries of the Rosary* for its subject. One day, while engaged in prayer, and reflecting in what way he could best please his celestial patroness, he felt an irresistible desire to take upon himself the vow of perpetual chastity, which vow was in reality made by him in the ninth year of his age, in presence of the miraculous picture of the Annunciation. So faithfully did he keep his vow, that those who knew his inner life well, affirm that not only did he preserve his chastity pure and unsullied, but that he was wholly free from every temptation of the flesh and spirit. By endowing him with this extraordinary grace, our Blessed Lady testified how well-pleasing to her Divine Son, and to herself, was this resolve of St. Aloysius. His greatest pleasure was to visit some church specially dedicated to the Blessed Virgin. From the time he was twelve years old, Aloysius fasted every Saturday, and on the Vigils of our Blessed Lady's Feasts; taking nothing, save bread and water. In all his needs he had recourse to her; entreating her to aid him, that he might learn what his true vocation was (as we all know, he became a member of the Society of Jesus). He begged her to remove the hindrances he experienced on his father's part; which prayer was also granted. He

always believed that the best way to serve and please Mary, consists in imitating her holiness of life. Hence his unwearying and persistent efforts to perfect himself in that virtue which shows forth so brilliantly in our Blessed Lady herself. How ardent his love of poverty! How deep his humility! How perfect his obedience, his purity, his love to God and man! His eyes were ever fixed on Jesus and Mary, whom he strove to glorify by the practice of the aforenamed virtues. He died in the 24th year of his age; young in years, but rich in purity. He is now with Jesus and Mary, whom he loved so tenderly. Happy Aloysius! And happy they who follow in his steps! In order that we may be of that happy band, let us pray, with the Church: O God, the distributor of heavenly gifts, who in the angelical Aloysius, didst unite a wonderful innocence of life with equally wonderful penance; grant through his merits and prayers, that we, who have not followed him in innocence, may imitate him in penance, through Jesus Christ our Lord. Amen.

PRACTICE.

Out of love to Jesus and Mary, bear the Cross now laid on thee by thy Lord.

29TH DAY.

THE ASSUMPTION.

1ST PART.

Mary's departure from earth was especially remarkable; and that, on account of her unworldly spirit, her longing for Heaven, and her love for God.

1. HER UNWORLDLY SPIRIT. Mary knew, far better than others, the transitoriness and worthlessness of all terrestrial things; earth never had any hold on her affections: her departure was calm and peaceful, for she was bound by no earthly fetters. Such will not be their case, who cling to terrestrial things. Their end will be full of pain, bitterness, terror and anguish.

2. MARY'S LONGING FOR HEAVEN. Tradition tells us that Mary had attained the age of 60, or 62. Her exile here below seemed protracted indeed; she yearned for Heaven, the sole object of her desires. Hence, death, to her, was a most welcome messenger, since it would introduce her to her eternal home. Words fail to describe the

intensity of her desire to enter that celestial abode, on whose threshold she was standing. It is sad for us that we cling so lovingly to this miserable land of exile; that we love this vale of tears, and almost wholly forget our true home, the heavenly Jerusalem.

3. MARY'S LOVE TO GOD. We may truly say that divine love was the cause of Mary's death. Picture that blessed one reposing on her poor couch, her hands folded on her breast, her eyes raised to Heaven, her heart glowing with most fervent love to God! Happy transit from time to eternal bliss! What a blessed death to die! May our last breath, like hers, be an act of perfect love to God! Then what a happy death will ours be!

PRAYER.

Queen of Patriarchs, Queen of Prophets, pray for us.

O Mary, Queen of Heaven and Earth, by thy simple, firm, unvacillating trust in God, by thy belief in the Redemption and the other Divine promises, thou hast far excelled all the Patriarchs. By thy clear insight into the Divine Mysteries, by the liveliness, submissiveness, and constancy of thy faith, thou hast excelled the Prophets,

and art, with justice, styled their Queen. The hearts of all yearned for thy advent as heralding in the dawn of the Sun of Righteousness. Thou art the Queen of Heaven, and Sovereign Mistress of all created beings. Obtain us the lively faith and ardent hope that animated the saints, so that we may grow in love, persevere to the end, and hereafter, in company with Patriarchs, Prophets, and all the Elect of God, glorify thee, together with the Father, Son, and Holy Ghost, through all eternity. Amen.

EXAMPLE.

St. Stephen, King of Hungary.

This Saint, the first King of Hungary, was a zealous and devoted child of Mary. He was born in Hungary, in the year 969. His father, Geisa, fourth Duke of Hungary, and his mother, Sarloth, were heathens by birth, but had been converted to Christianity before the birth of their son. Stephen was carefully trained in the Christian religion, and in the practice of all virtue. On succeeding to the throne, his first care was to introduce Christianity throughout the length and breadth of the land, and utterly destroy every vestige of heathenism. This was no easy undertaking, since the

majority of his subjects were heathens. But he placed all his trust in God, whose cause he had undertaken to defend. And what may not a king effect, who earnestly desires and perseveringly strives to do good, trusting in God alone? In order the better to ensure the Divine assistance, he had constant recourse to the Blessed Virgin, whom from infancy he had so tenderly loved; and by her aid he overcame all obstacles, and succeeded in promulgating the Gospel throughout his territories. In the year 1000 he sent an embassy to Rome, commending his now Christian country to the care of the Sovereign Pontiff, whom he entreated to confer on him the title of King. Pope Silvester II. granted his request, and sent him the royal crown, by the hands of the ambassadors. He also sent the new king a cross, as a mark of his apostolic office, and in recognition of his zeal in propagating the Gospel, which cross the Sovereign Pontiff most graciously allowed him to have borne before him, especially in time of war. Stephen was crowned with the greatest pomp; he selected the Mother of God as the *patroness of his kingdom*, and erected a splendid church in her honour, in the town of Alba, named, on account of his residing there, the royal city, or *Alba regalis*, and which at the present time is known as *Stuhlweiszenburg*.

Since then our Blessed Lady has ever been honoured by the Hungarians as their Patroness. Stephen was a valiant general, but wholly unambitious; he never waged war for the sake of territorial aggrandisement; but whenever the cause of religion or his subjects' welfare was endangered, he was ever ready to draw the sword for their protection. Success always crowned his arms; but he never took the field without having first begged the Divine blessing, and Mary's aid. In the hour of danger, her name was ever on his lips; to her mighty protection he commended himself, in order that he might make diligent progress in virtue, and be well-pleasing in her Divine Son's sight; in all his enterprises, Mary was his consolation, joy, and the source of his tranquillity. We will cite a touching instance of this. The saintly monarch had disguised himself one day, in order to distribute alms. But some of the objects of his generosity were coarse, rough persons; they attacked the king, threw him on the ground, shamefully maltreated him, robbed him of his money, and then ran hastily away. The Saint suffered this ignominious treatment with the greatest patience; he even rejoiced that he was thus permitted to augment his merits, and, turning to Mary, his celestial patroness, thus addressed her: "See, O Queen of Heaven, my be-

loved Mistress, how these people treat him whom thou hast permitted to wear the crown. If they were foes, I should know how to avenge my honour; but as they are the subjects of thy Divine Son and my Redeemer, I joyfully endure this at their hands." What magnanimity lies couched beneath these words, and what love and veneration to our Blessed Lady! After labouring most zealously, his life long, in the spread of the Gospel and in promoting Mary's honour, he at last saw his final hour draw nigh. Assembling his nobles, he urgently entreated them to preserve peace, to defend the cause of religion, to pay due respect to the Holy See, to keep the commandments, and place implicit, child-like trust in Mary. He gave up the ghost on the 15th August, 1038, on the Feast of the Assumption, the chief feast of her whom, in life, he had so deeply reverenced, and whose presence he was now about to enjoy throughout eternity. What a consolatory thought it is when they who are placed in authority can conscientiously say that they have led their subjects to God. To attain this blessed result, nought is so availing as heartfelt love and devotion to Mary.

Practice.

Be patient under suffering. Remember Jesus; without patience thou canst never attain Heaven. For Mary's sake, forgive all who have injured, or offended thee.

30TH DAY.

THE ASSUMPTION.

1ST PART.

Mary's assumption, a source of joy to the faithful. Angels escorted her to Heaven. Her reception by her Divine Son.

1. EARTH REJOICED. Tradition says that after Mary's sacred remains had been most reverently entombed by the faithful, angelic songs were heard proceeding from the sepulchre, during the space of three days; and, on opening the tomb, nought was to be seen save the grave-clothes in which the sacred body had been enveloped—the body itself was nowhere to be found. It was revealed to the faithful, that this living Ark of the Covenant, this body in which Jesus dwelt, had been assumed into Heaven. With what glad hymns of joy must these tidings have been welcomed by them! Let us unite our congratulations to theirs, and thank God for the honour conferred on Mary. Also let us remember that she, whose entrance into Heaven we celebrate to-day, is our Mother,

and that she is gone to prepare a place for us, her children.

2. THE ANGELIC ESCORT. The blessed spirits forsook Heaven, in order to hasten to meet their Queen, and escort her to Heaven, amid triumphant songs of joy. God grant that thy angel-guardian may one day come to meet and receive thy soul, and conduct it to Heaven. Beg this grace, through Mary's intercession.

3. MARY'S RECEPTION. The Divine Redeemer came forward to welcome His mother, to receive her into eternal glory, and conduct her to her exalted throne. Leaning on her beloved Son, *(innixa super dilectum suum)* Mary passed through the angelic choirs and the ranks of the Elect. Happy he who places his hope in Jesus, who casts himself in His arms, and loves and reverences His Divine Mother. Such an one may confidently hope to attain eternal glory. O Mary, thou blessed, loving Mother, compassionate us, thy orphan children. Draw us to thyself, and may we hereafter share thy bliss.

PRAYER.

Queen of Apostles, Queen of Martyrs, pray for us!

O Mary! apostles and martyrs have embarked on the most arduous enterprises; endured most

poignant sufferings; and shed their blood for the glory of God. But thou hast done more; no sufferings ever equalled thine. By thy example and thy exhortations, thou didst cheer, comfort, and strengthen the apostles. The degree and duration of thy sufferings, thy constancy and thy love, were unsurpassed, so that thou art rightly named Queen of Apostles, and Queen of Martyrs. Win us grace rightly to comprehend the happiness of suffering for Jesus, and strength to bear our cross patiently, as thou didst bear thine. Amen.

Example.

St. Stanislaus Kostka.

In deep, tender devotion to our Blessed Lady, St. Stanislaus Kostka has but few equals; and few have received so many, and so great proofs of her maternal love and care. As a child, Stanislaus was more like an angel than a human being: he was so sensitive and pure-hearted, that he would faint on hearing an unseemly, or ambiguous word. While quite a boy, his parents sent him, with his elder brother Paul to Vienna, to be educated at the Jesuits' College. As this College was done away with on the death of Ferdinand I., the pupils were obliged to take up their abode in private houses.

To Stanislaus' great grief, he and his brother had to live in a Lutheran family. Here he had much to endure at the hands of his brother, who grew more and more careless and thoughtless, and to whom the quiet holy life of his brother was a silent reproach. Stanislaus fell dangerously ill, and asked for the last Sacraments. As a variety of pretexts were alleged for not complying with his request, he looked to God and his glorious patroness for aid. His heart's desire was at once granted. St. Barbara, for whom he had always entertained great devotion, accompanied by two angels, brought him Holy Communion, that true Bread of Life, and Mary appeared in all her loving tenderness, to comfort and cheer him; she also placed her Divine Son, under the form of a little child, within his arms, permitting Him to repose there for some time. Stanislaus, beside himself with holy joy and rapture, had no thought save of Jesus, and of the blessedness awaiting him in Heaven, where he would soon forever enjoy the presence of his Divine Lord. But Mary revealed to him that this bliss was not yet to be his; that he must do more to merit this grace; and that nothing would so potently contribute to this happy result, as unswerving obedience to her Divine Son's Will, adding: "Therefore thou must enter the Society

which bears His name; such is my Son's desire regarding thee, and, in His stead, I enjoin thee to comply". This miraculous revelation occurred in Vienna, in the Court Presbytery, where the chamber Stanislaus occupied has been converted into the well-known Stanislaus Chapel, to which, during the Octave of the Saint's Feast, numbers of the faithful are wont to resort. Stanislaus had scarcely recovered when he hastened to obey the commands of Jesus and Mary. After surmounting various obstacles, he succeeded in obtaining admission into the Novitiate in Rome. He never forgot that he owed his vocation to Mary; and so fervent was his love, so deep his trust, that his fellow-novices believed the surest way of obtaining any grace from Mary, was for Stanislaus to unite his supplications to theirs. His zeal for Mary's glory induced him to extract from works of the Fathers, or other pious authors, all the sublime and glorious things they had written in Mary's praise. When conversing, he always said something in our Blessed Lady's honour; hence, many sought his society, that they might hear him converse on this theme; for in addition to what he had culled from various works, his own thoughts were so striking, edifying, and expressed with such humility and fervour, that his hearers were deeply impressed,

and devotion was awakened in every breast. He always called Mary his Mother, and such she was truly to him; so fervent was his affection for her, that a celebrated individual was so astonished in listening to him, that he remarked to Francis Borgia (the General of the Order, at that time), that his manner and his language, when conversing on this his favourite theme, partook more of Heaven than Earth. So intense and ardent was his love for that Celestial Mother, that he was impatient to quit this place of exile; his prayers were answered, and the blessing of an early death vouchsafed him. He had been ten months a novice, when he was conversing, early in August, with a Jesuit Priest, respecting Mary's Assumption, and the joy with which that Feast must be celebrated in Heaven, adding: "I confidently hope to spend the next anniversary of this Feast with those blessed ones". With child-like simplicity and love, he wrote a letter to the Blessed Virgin, entreating her to grant him this favour; he wore the letter on his breast on receiving Holy Communion on St. Laurence's Day (10th August), earnestly beseeching his beloved mother that he might soon be called from this vale of tears, to behold her Heavenly Glory. Up to this time Stanislaus was in perfect health, so that no trace

of indisposition, much less of any dangerous malady, could be discerned in him. But, ere the day closed, he began to feel unwell. Although the symptoms were not grave, the Superior ordered him to bed, and as the saintly youth entered the dormitory, he made the sign of the Cross over the bed, saying: "I shall never rise from this bed". And on the Superior visiting him a little later on, he said quite confidently, that he fully believed our Blessed Lady had granted him the favour to die before her Feast, so that he might celebrate it with the Saints in Heaven. The result proved the truth of these words. His illness did not assume a serious character; and even on the morning of the 14th of August, the physicians saw nothing alarming in his condition; but, after mid-day, the symptoms assumed a graver aspect. The last Sacraments were administered to Stanislaus, who, out of humility received them, extended on the floor. He then passed some time in prayer; he held in his hand a picture of our Blessed Lady, which he often kissed with the most tender affection; his Rosary encircled his arm, and on some one asking why he wore it now that he was unable to tell his beads, he replied: "True, I cannot tell my beads; but it is a great comfort to me to see them, because they remind me of my

beloved Mother." After midnight, Stanislaus felt his last hour draw nigh, and prayed with still deeper fervour. He beheld the Queen of Heaven approach, surrounded by a multitude of saintly Virgins, to bear him hence to eternal joy; soon after this, at three in the morning of the 15th August, 1568, he departed this life, at the age of eighteen. Let us love Mary as Stanislaus loved her, so that she may assist us in our dying hour, and receive our soul as she received his. Also let us beg of her, grace to die on one of her Festivals.

Practice.

Imitate Mary's example, and, from love to her, suffer and do all that God demands from thee; saying often: "Behold the Handmaid of the Lord, be it done to me according to thy word".

31st DAY.

3rd PART.

The Blessed Virgin was crowned with a triple Diadem, denoting her glory, her guardianship of the human race, and her power over the infernal spirits.

1. HER CROWN OF GLORY. When Mary had reached the throne of the most Blessed Trinity, the Eternal Father (according to the picturesque language of Holy Scripture), crowned her with glory, robed her with the sun, gave her the moon for her footstool, girt her brow with a diadem of twelve stars, and, as Queen of Saints and Angels, exalted her on the glorious throne prepared for her from the beginning. When will that happy moment dawn when we too shall reach Heaven, and present our homage to our glorious Queen? Happy we, if such bliss await us hereafter!

2. HER CROWN, AS GUARDIAN OF THE HUMAN RACE. Inasmuch as Mary shares our human nature, it pleased the Eternal Word to appoint her our guardian, so that in all our needs we may ever have recourse to her who is our unfailing Advocate

with the Eternal Father.—So powerful and so loving is our Celestial Mother; yet how rarely do we turn to her for aid!

3. HER DOMINION OVER THE INFERNAL SPIRITS. The Holy Ghost, the love of the Father and the Son, that divine fire which melts the rocks, made His spouse participate in His Divine sway over Hell. As from the beginning she had crushed the Serpent's head, so now she was to exercise a still greater power over the hellish foe. Hence the name of Mary is so terrible to Satan and all the infernal spirits. In temptation, let us confidently invoke that name, and Satan will take his flight, and all his temptations vanish.

PRAYER.

Queen of Confessors, Queen of Virgins, pray for us.

O most exalted Queen of those noble souls who shrunk not from confessing thy Son in the eyes of the whole universe, and this, not only by word, but in deed also; who gloried to follow the Evangelic Counsels, who condemned the treasures of earth, its pomp, and pleasures, in order that they might enjoy closer union with their Divine Lord. In the steadfast pursuit of good, and in purity of heart, thou, O wondrous Mother, hast far excelled them

all. When all the rest gave way, thy faith remained unmovable. *Blessed art thou, inasmuch as thou hast believed!* Thou wast the first to unfurl the standard of Virginity. By thy example thou didst animate Confessors and Virgins, sustaining them in the dangerous struggle with the world, the flesh, and the devil. Aid us too, O mighty Queen! Strengthen us, make us steadfast in faith and purity, so that we may live as becomes the faithful disciples of thyself and thy Divine Son, and be well-pleasing in His sight and thine. Amen.

EXAMPLE.

St. Charles Borromeo.

St. Charles Borromeo, Cardinal, and Archbishop of Milan, had the most tender devotion to our Blessed Lady; he recited the Chaplet and the Angelic Salutation daily on his knees, and fasted, on bread and water, on the Vigils of her Feasts. He was surpassed by none in zeal and love to Mary. If he happened to be in the street when the Angelus sounded, he knelt down on the ground immediately, no matter how dirty it might be. One of the Chapels in his Cathedral was dedicated by him to our Blessed Lady, and the Confraternity of the Rosary established. On the First Sunday

in the month, a solemn procession took place, and an image of our Lady was carried round the Church. All the pious institutions founded by him (and they are numerous indeed!) he dedicated to the Mother of God, naming her their patroness. He also ordered that whenever Mary's name was uttered, it should be accompanied by the usual salutation. Also, that there should be a representation of our Lady over the chief entrance to all the Churches in his diocese, to remind the faithful that none can enter the heavenly Temple, save through the intercession of her whom the Church styles *the Gate of Heaven*.

PRACTICE.

Daily place yourself under Mary's protection, and renew this offering frequently throughout the day.

REMARK.

In order to conclude these devotions in a suitable manner, and profit by the practices of the following day, read paragraph seven of the Introduction.

CONCLUDING MEDITATION.

TO BE USED ON THE LAST DAY OF THE MONTH, OR ON THE FOLLOWING DAY.

In order to close the monthly devotion in a befitting manner, and profit by the same, consecrate your heart to the Blessed Mother of God, entreating her to inspire you with holy fear, unshaken confidence, and ardent love to God.

1. HOLY FEAR. The Holy Ghost says the *fear of God is the beginning of wisdom*. Therefore, if thou desirest to attain wisdom and divine knowledge, to serve and please God, and secure thy soul's salvation, let this holy fear of God be your guide in the road to perfection, for "*Blessed is the man who feareth the Lord and delighteth in his Law*". This holy fear banishes sin from the soul, fills the heart with gladness, and ensures eternal life. Therefore cast aside all human respect, and fear Him who has power to destroy both body and soul in hell; fear to displease Him who ever loads thee with His benefits,—thou canst incur no greater misfortune than this. Fear to offend Him who is the impersonation of all goodness, who merits thy never-dying affection, but

whom thou so often treatest with coldness and indifference! This holy fear was possessed by Mary, and that in such marked degree that she is named the *Mother of holy fear*. Entreat her to obtain thee this blessed gift of the Holy Ghost, and offer her thy heart, that she may teach thee the fear of the Lord.

2. UNSHAKEN CONFIDENCE. Hope in God is the distinguishing trait of the soul that trusts in Him. By hoping in God, we honour His Divine Omnipotence and goodness; and who has ever had deeper experience and knowledge of God's goodness and omnipotence than Mary had? To whom, then, shall we flee for this priceless gift, save to her who is rightly named *the Mother of holy hope*. Often thy courage fails, thou art disquieted by a thousand fears. Didst thou but address thyself to Mary, what peace and succour thou wouldst experience! Offer her now thy whole heart, place thyself beneath her protection; if Mary accepts thee, thou hast truly nought to fear.

3. FERVENT LOVE. Mary loved God with deeper ardour than the cherubim, seraphim, and all created beings have experienced, or ever can experience. Like the sun, which grows ever brighter and brighter until he attains his noonday splendour, so, from the first dawn of consciousness, Mary's love to her

Creator grew more and more fervent, attaining its zenith at the moment of her departure from earth. No cloud ever dimmed her love, no imperfection marred its purity; she loved with her whole heart, and her affection grew ever deeper and deeper still. Alas! how cold are our hearts, how indifferent we are! Let us entreat Mary to compassionate us. Let us offer our hearts to her, that she may melt them, and attune them to Divine Love. Daily let us supplicate her that we may grow in love, and hereafter love God throughout eternity. O Mary, teach me to love thee, and love thy Son; may I love in time, so that I may love throughout eternity! This is the blessing I desire above all others, and entreat it, in the name of thy Son, JESUS CHRIST. Amen.

PRAYER.

Queen of Saints, Queen conceived without sin, pray for us!

Queen of Heaven and Earth, thou didst magnify God and love Him with a love exceeding that of the Saints, and now thy glory far surpasses theirs. The Saints gaze in admiration at thy virtues and thy perfection; they praise and glorify thee as their Queen. O tender Mother! despise not our

petitions; receive our homage, veneration, and love. Be thou our Queen; we flee to thy mighty protection; to thee do we dedicate ourselves, and all that we have. Be thou the ruler of our destiny; command us as thou wilt. In thee do we place our whole trust; for though thou art our Queen, thou art also our gracious loving Mother. To thee do we commit ourselves, body, soul, and spirit, with all we have and are. We lay this offering at thy feet; show thyself our Mother, both in life and death, O clement, O loving, O sweet Virgin Mary! Amen.

EXAMPLE.

Mary, the Patroness of Austria.

In the year 1647, Ferdinand III., Emperor of Austria, was hard beset by his foes, and especially so by the Swedes. Not only the Catholic faith in his own domains, but the liberty and independence of Germany, were exposed to great danger. The pious monarch, seeing himself deserted by his former allies, in order to save both Church and State, hastened to place himself beneath the powerful protection of her who is rightly designated the *Help of Christians*. Therefore he resolved to commit himself, his family, and his country, to

Mary's special guardianship, making a solemn vow to erect a monument to her honour within the Hof-platz. As soon as the Emperor's intentions became known, they were hailed with joy by the magistracy and citizens of Vienna, by the Austrian nobility, clergy, and by the whole of the populace. It was unanimously decreed that each individual should, in his own name and that of his posterity, bind himself by a vow to observe annually, throughout all coming generations, the Feast of the Immaculate Conception, on December 8, and to celebrate the same with all possible solemnity; and that Mary should be proclaimed Patroness and defender of Austria. The 18th of May, 1647, was set apart for the inauguration of this festival. Nothing could exceed its beauty. The Court, nobility, clergy, citizens, the whole country, all ranks and classes, desired to take part in this auspicious ceremony. When the much-desired day began to dawn, crowds thronged the streets and squares of the capital. At eight o'clock in the morning, the Emperor, in solemn pomp, proceeded on foot from the Augustinian Church to that of the Jesuits, in which latter edifice the festival was to be held. The Emperor was surrounded by his whole Court. At his right and left were Ferdinand IV., then King of Bohemia, and the Arch-

duchess Maria Anna, betrothed to the King of Spain. The suite was composed of the Papal Nuncio, the Spanish and Venetian Representatives, all the foreign Ambassadors, nobility, clergy, regular and secular, and persons of every rank and condition in life. In the Hof-platz, in front of the newly-erected monument, an impressive sermon was preached in Our Blessed Lady's honour and in explanation of the Festival. Philip Frederic, Prince-Bishop of Vienna, celebrated High Mass in the before-named Church. On receiving the kiss of peace, in accordance to custom, from the Sub-deacon, the Emperor proceeded to the High Altar, handed his sword to the High Chamberlain, and kneeling humbly in front of the altar, whilst the pontificating Bishop faced him, holding the Sacred Host in his hand, in a loud voice pronounced the following vow:—" Almighty and eternal God by Whom kings reign, and from Whom all power proceedeth! I, Ferdinand, humbly prostrate myself before Thy Divine Majesty, and in my own name and in that of my successors, as well as in the name of this renowned Austrian Province, I to-day elect and nominate the Immaculate Virgin-Mother of Thy Son as Sovereign Patroness of this Archduchy. Moreover, I vow and promise that the Festival of the Immaculate Conception, which

falls on December 8, shall be celebrated annually throughout the whole Province as a day of obligation, and that the preceding day shall be observed as one of fasting and abstinence. I entreat Thee, O Lord, Most High, Ruler of Heaven and Earth, who acceptest the homage offered to Thy Mother, as if it were offered to Thee, mercifully receive this vow which Thou hast inspired me to make, and stretch forth Thy Hand for my defence, and for the defence of my house and that of the people entrusted to my care. Amen."

When the Sovereign had made his vows, he received Holy Communion at the hands of the Prince-Bishop, and then returned to his throne. After Mass, the Emperor and his suite proceeded from the Church to the spot where the monument in Mary's honour had been erected, and which was consecrated by the Prince-Bishop amid hymns of praise, thanksgiving, and volleys of artillery. In the evening, the whole Place, especially the splendid Column, and our Blessed Lady's image, were brilliantly illumined, and the Emperor, with the Princes and Princesses re-visited the joyful scene. The Litany of Loretto and other hymns of praise were sung before the Statue of our Lady, and at the close of the Festival, Benediction was given by the Prince-Bishop. Thus ended this glorious day, and the confidence placed in the

Immaculate Virgin Mother was not in vain. The Emperor's former allies returned to his side. The God of Hosts sent torrents of rain and deep floods which barred the advance of the Swedish troops, who were just meditating an invasion of Upper Austria! Repulsed and defeated by the Imperial arms, the foe was at last compelled to sue for peace. Thus was Austria saved by Mary's powerful patronage. The fine monument with its various sculptures which Ferdinand III. had erected in the centre of the Hof-platz, reminds the Viennese of the present day, as well as every Austrian subject, that Mary is their Patroness and their Protectress. She is also the Patroness of every Christian. What an encouraging and consolatory thought that is! If we trust perseveringly in Mary, honour and invoke her, and strive to please her by the steadfastness of our faith, and the purity of our life and conversation, she will ever act a mother's part to us and protect us in all danger and adversity.

Practice.

Cherish within your breast an ardent devotion to the most holy Immaculate Heart of Mary, and pray for the conversion of sinners.

For Act of Consecration, see page xiii.

MORNING PRAYERS.

Awaking in the Morning, say:

O my God, my only good, the author of my being and my last end, I offer Thee my heart. Praise, honour, and glory be to Thee for ever and ever.

At rising.

I will arise from this bed of sleep to adore my God, and to labour for the salvation of my soul. Oh, may I rise on the last day to life everlasting!

When clothed, kneel and say:

✠ In the name of the Father, and of the Son, and of the Holy Ghost. Amen.

Come, O Holy Ghost, fill the hearts of thy faithful, and kindle in them the fire of thy love.

Place yourself in the presence of God.

Most holy and adorable Trinity, one God in three persons, I believe that Thou art here present; I adore Thee with the deepest humility, and render to Thee, with my whole heart, the homage which is due to Thy sovereign Majesty.

Thank God, and offer yourself to Him.

My God, I most humbly thank Thee for all the

favours Thou hast bestowed upon me up to the present moment. I give Thee thanks from the bottom of my heart that Thou hast created me after Thine own image and likeness, that Thou hast redeemed me by the precious blood of Thy dear Son, and that Thou hast preserved me and brought me safe to the beginning of another day. I offer to Thee, O Lord, my whole being, and in particular all my thoughts, words, actions, and sufferings of this day. I consecrate them all to the glory of Thy name, beseeching Thee that through the infinite merits of Jesus Christ my Saviour they may all find acceptance in Thy sight. May Thy divine love animate them, and may they all tend to Thy greater glory.

Resolve to avoid sin and to practise holiness.

Adorable Jesus, my Saviour and Master, model of all perfection, I resolve and will endeavour this day to imitate Thy example, to be like Thee mild, humble, chaste, zealous, charitable, and resigned. I will redouble my efforts that I may not fall this day into any of those sins which I have heretofore committed *(here you may name any besetting sin)*, and which I sincerely desire to forsake.

Implore the necessary Graces.

O my God, Thou knowest my poverty and weakness, and that I am unable to do anything good without Thee; deny me not, O God, the help of

Thy grace; proportion it to my necessities; give me strength to avoid everything evil which Thou forbiddest, and to practice the good which Thou hast commanded; and enable me to bear patiently all the trials which it may please Thee to send me.

Our Father. Hail Mary. I believe. I confess to Almighty God, &c.

[A Litany, or the "Veni Creator," may be added.]

An Act of Faith.

O my God, I firmly believe all that Thou hast revealed, and which the holy Catholic Church proposes to me to be believed, because Thou art truth itself, which can neither deceive nor be deceived. In this faith I desire to live and die.

An Act of Hope.

O my God, relying on Thy gracious promises, I hope, by the merits of Jesus Christ, for the pardon of my sins, grace to serve Thee faithfully in this life by doing the good works which Thou hast commanded, and eternal happiness in the world to come, through Jesus Christ our Lord.

An Act of Love.

O my God, I love Thee with my whole heart, and above all things, because Thou art infinitely good in Thyself and infinitely to be loved; and for the love of Thee I love my neighbour as myself.

An Act of Contrition.

O my God, I repent with my whole heart of having offended Thee; I detest my sins for the love of Thee; I firmly resolve never to offend Thee again, and by the help of Thy grace to avoid every occasion of sin.

Ask the Prayers of the Saints.

Holy Virgin, Mother of God, my Mother and Patroness, I place myself under thy protection, I throw myself with confidence into the arms of thy compassion. Be to me, O Mother of Mercy, my refuge in distress, my consolation under suffering, my advocate with thy adorable Son, now and at the hour of my death.

Angel of heaven, my faithful and loving guide, obtain for me grace to be obedient to thy holy inspirations, and so to direct my steps that I may not in anything depart from the will and commandments of my God.

O great Saint, whose name I bear, protect me, pray for me, that like you I may serve God faithfully on earth, and glorify Him eternally with you in heaven. Amen.

Act of Resignation to the Will of God.

May the most just, most high, and most amiable will of God be done, praised, and eternally exalted in all things. Amen.

LITANY OF LORETTO.

Ant. Sub tuum præsidium confugimus, sancta Dei Genitrix, nostras deprecationes ne despicias in necessitatibus nostris; sed a periculis cunctis libera nos semper, Virgo gloriosa et benedicta.

Ant. We fly to thy patronage, O holy Mother of God, despise not our petitions in our necessities; but deliver us always from all dangers, O glorious and blessed Virgin.

Kyrie eleison.	Lord have mercy.
Kyrie eleison.	*Lord have mercy.*
Christe eleison.	Christ have mercy.
Christe eleison.	*Christ have mercy.*
Kyrie eleison.	Lord have mercy.
Kyrie eleison.	*Lord have mercy.*
Christe audi nos.	Christ hear us.
Christe exaudi nos.	*Christ graciously hear us.*
Pater de cœlis Deus,	God the Father of heaven,
Fili Redemptor mundi Deus,	God the Son, Redeemer of the world,
Spiritus Sancte Deus,	God the Holy Ghost,
Sancta Trinitas, unus Deus,	Holy Trinity, one God,
Sancta Maria,	Holy Mary,
Sancti Dei Genetrix,	Holy Mother of God,
Sancta Virgo virginum,	Holy Virgin of virgins,
Mater Christi,	Mother of Christ,
Mater divinæ gratiæ,	Mother of divine grace,
Mater purissima,	Mother most pure,
Mater castissima,	Mother most chaste,
Mater inviolata,	Mother inviolate.
Mater intemerata,	Mother undefiled,
Mater amabilis,	Mother most amiable,
Mater admirabilis,	Mother most admirable,
Mater Creatoris,	Mother of our Creator,
Mater Salvatoris,	Mother of our Saviour,
Virgo prudentissima,	Virgin most prudent,
Virgo veneranda,	Virgin most venerable,
Virgo prædicanda,	Virgin most renowned,

(Latin side: *Miserere nobis.* / *Ora pro nobis.*)
(English side: *Have mercy on us.* / *Pray for us.*)

Virgo potens,	Virgin most powerful,
Virgo clemens,	Virgin most merciful,
Virgo fidelis,	Virgin most faithful,
Speculum justitiæ,	Mirror of justice,
Sedes sapientiæ,	Seat of Wisdom,
Causa nostræ lætitiæ,	Cause of our joy,
Vas spirituale,	Spiritual Vessel,
Vas honorabile,	Vessel of honour,
Vas insigne devotionis,	Vessel of singular devotion,
Rosa mystica,	Mystical Rose,
Turris Davidica,	Tower of David,
Turris eburnea,	Tower of ivory,
Domus aurea,	House of gold,
Fœderis arca,	Ark of the covenant,
Janua cœli,	Gate of heaven,
Stella matutina,	Morning star,
Salus infirmorum,	Health of the sick,
Refugium peccatorum,	Refuge of sinners,
Consolatrix afflictorum,	Comforter of the afflicted.
Auxilium Christianorum,	Help of Christians,
Ora pro nobis.	*Pray for us.*
Regina Angelorum,	Queen of angels,
Regina Patriarcharum,	Queen of Patriarchs,
Regina Prophetarum,	Queen of Prophets,
Regina Apostolorum,	Queen of Apostles,
Regina Martyrum,	Queen of Martyrs,
Regina Confessorum,	Queen of Confessors,
Regina Virginum,	Queen of Virgins,
Regina Sanctorum omnium,	Queen of all Saints,
Regina sine labe originali concepta,	Queen conceived without original sin,
Regina sanctissimi Rosarii,	Queen of the most holy Rosary,
Ora pro nobis.	*Pray for us.*
Agnus Dei, qui tollis peccata mundi,	Lamb of God, Who takest away the sins of the world,
Parce nobis, Domine,	*Spare us, O Lord.*
Agnus Dei, qui tollis peccata mundi,	Lamb of God, Who takest away the sins of the world,
Exaudi nos, Domine.	*Graciously hear us, O Lord.*
Agnus Dei, qui tollis peccata mundi,	Lamb of God, Who takest away the sins of the world,
Miserere nobis.	*Have mercy on us.*
Christe audi nos.	Christ hear us.
Christe exaudi nos.	*Christ graciously hear us.*

Ant. Sub tuum præsidium confugimus, sancta Dei Genitrix. Nostras deprecationes ne despicias in necessitatibus nostris; sed a periculis cunctis libera nos semper, Virgo gloriosa et benedicta.

V. Ora pro nobis, sancta Dei Genitrix.

R. Ut digni efficiamur promissionibus Christi.

Oremus.

Gratiam tuam quæsumus, Domine, mentibus nostris infunde; ut qui angelo nuntiante, Christi Filii, tui incarnationem cognovimus, per passionem ejus et crucem ad resurrectionis gloriam perducamur. Per eundem Christum Dominum nostrum. Amen.

V. Divinum auxilium maneat semper nobiscum.
R. Amen.

Ant. We fly to thy patronage, O holy Mother of God. Despise not our petitions in our necessities; but deliver us always from all dangers, O glorious and blessed Virgin.

V. Pray for us, O holy Mother of God.

R. That we may be made worthy of the promises of Christ.

Let us pray.

Pour forth, we beseech Thee, O Lord, Thy grace into our hearts; that we, to whom the incarnation of Christ Thy Son was made known by the message of an angel, may by His passion and cross be brought to the glory of His resurrection. Through the same Christ our Lord. Amen.

V. May the divine assistance remain always with us.
R. Amen.

PRAYERS FOR NIGHT.

In the name of the Father, and of the Son, and of the Holy Ghost. Amen.

Blessed be the holy and undivided Trinity, now and for ever. Amen.

Our Father, &c. Hail Mary, &c.

I believe in God, &c.

Come, O holy Spirit, fill the hearts of Thy faithful, and kindle in them the fire of Thy love.

V. Send forth Thy Spirit, and they shall be created.

R. And thou shalt renew the face of the earth.

Let us place ourselves in the presence of God, and give him thanks for all the benefits which we have received from him, particularly this day.

O my God, I firmly believe that Thou art here, and perfectly seest me, and that Thou observest all my actions, all my thoughts, and the most secret motions of my heart. Thou watchest over me with an incomparable love, every moment bestowing favours, and preserving me from evil. Blessed be Thy holy name, and may all creatures bless Thy goodness for the benefits which I have ever received from Thee, and particularly this day. May the saints and angels supply my defect in rendering

Thee due thanks. Never permit me to be so base and wicked, as to repay Thy bounties with ingratitude, and Thy blessings with offences and injuries.

Let us ask of our Lord Jesus Christ grace to discover the sins which we have committed this day; and beg of him a true sorrow for them, and a sincere repentance.

O my Lord Jesus Christ, judge of the living and the dead, before Whom I must appear one day to give an exact account of my whole life; enlighten me, I beseech Thee, and give me an humble and contrite heart, that I may see wherein I have offended Thine infinite Majesty; and judge myself now with such a just severity, that then Thou mayest judge me with mercy and clemency.

Let us here examine what sins we have committed this day, by thought, word, deed, or omission.

(If nothing occur to your mind, wherein you have offended, renew your sorrow for the sins of your past life.)

Let us conceive a great sorrow for having offended God.

O my God, I detest these and all other sins, which I have committed against Thy divine Majesty. I am extremely sorry that I have offended Thee, because Thou art infinitely good, and sin displeaseth Thee. I love Thee with my whole heart, and firmly purpose, by the help of Thy grace, never more to offend Thee. I resolve to avoid the occasions of sin; I will confess my sins, and will endeavour to make satisfaction for them. Have mercy on me, O God, have mercy, and pardon me, a wretched sinner. In the name of Thy beloved Son, Jesus, I humbly beg of Thee, so to wash me

with His precious blood, that my sins may be entirely remitted.

Let us endeavour, as much as possible, to put ourselves in the dispositions in which we desire to be found at the hour of death.

O my God, I accept of death as a homage and adoration which I owe to thy divine Majesty, and as a punishment justly due to my sins; in union with the death of my dear Redeemer, and as the only means of coming to Thee, my beginning and last end.

I firmly believe all the sacred truths which the Catholic Church believeth and teacheth, because Thou hast revealed them. And by the assistance of Thy holy grace, I am resolved to live and die in the communion of this thy church.

Relying upon Thy goodness, power, and promises, I hope to obtain pardon of my sins, and life everlasting, through the merits of Thy Son, Jesus Christ, my only Redeemer, and by the intercession of His blessed mother, and all the saints.

I love Thee with all my heart and soul, and desire to love Thee as the blessed do in heaven. I adore all the designs of Thy divine Providence, resigning myself entirely to Thy will.

I also love my neighbour for Thy sake, as I love myself: I sincerely forgive all who have injured me, and ask pardon of all whom I have injured.

I renounce the devil, with all his works; the

world, with all its pomps; the flesh, with all its temptations.

I desire to be dissolved, and to be with Christ. Father, into Thy hands I commend my spirit.

R. Lord Jesus, receive my soul.

May the blessed Virgin Mary, St. Joseph, and all the saints, pray for us to our Lord, that we may be preserved this night from sin and all evils. Amen.

Blessed St. Michael, defend us in the day of battle, that we may not be lost at the dreadful judgment. Amen.

O my good Angel, whom God, by His divine mercy, hath appointed to be my guardian, enlighten and protect me, direct and govern me this night. Amen.

May Almighty God have mercy on us, and forgive us our sins, and bring us to life everlasting. Amen.

May the Almighty and merciful Lord grant us pardon, absolution, and remission of all our sins. Amen.

V. Vouchsafe, O Lord, this night,
R. To keep us without sin.
V. Have mercy on us, O Lord.
R. Have mercy upon us.
V. Let Thy mercy, be upon us, O Lord.
R. As we have hoped in Thee.
V. O Lord, hear our prayer.
R. And let our cry come to Thee.

LET US PRAY.

Visit, we beseech Thee, O Lord, this house and family, and drive far from it all snares of the enemy; let Thy holy angels dwell herein, who may keep us in peace, and may Thy blessing be always upon us: through our Lord Jesus Christ. Amen.

May our Lord bless us, and preserve us from all evil, and bring us to life everlasting; and may the souls of the faithful departed, through the mercy of God, rest in peace. Amen.

Before you go to bed, read a chapter in the Scriptures, or some spiritual book; forecast with yourself the subject of the next morning's meditation, and think upon it whilst you are undressing yourself; when you compose yourself in your bed, think on your grave, and how quickly death, of which sleep is an image, will be with you, and what your sentiments will then be of all worldly vanities.

Offer up to God your sleep, resigning yourself to it in acquiescence with His holy will; and that by this repose of nature, you may recover new vigour to serve Him. Wish that every breath you are to take this night may be an act of praise and love of the divine Majesty, like the happy breathings of the angels and saints, who never sleep; and so compose yourself to rest in the arms of your Saviour. If you wake in the night, renew the offering of yourself to God, and aspire to Him; *My soul hath desired thee in the night.*—Isaias xxvi. 9.

DEVOTIONS FOR MASS.

In the name of the Father, and of the Son, and of the Holy Ghost. Amen.

A Prayer at the beginning of Mass.

O Almighty Lord of Heaven and Earth, behold I, a wretched sinner, presume to appear before Thee this day, to offer up to Thee by the hands of our High Priest, Jesus Christ, Thy Son, the Sacrifice of His body and blood, in union with the sacrifice which He offered to thee upon the cross: first, for thine own honour, praise, adoration, aud glory; secondly, in remembrance of His death and passion; thirdly, in thanksgiving for all thy blessings bestowed on Him and on His whole Church, whether triumphant in Heaven or militant on earth, and especially for those bestowed on me, the most unworthy of all; fourthly, for obtaining pardon and remission of all my sin, and for those of all others, whether living or dead, for whom I ought to pray; and lastly, for obtaining all graces aud blessing both for myself, and for Thy whole Church; Oh! be Thou pleased to assist me in such manner by Thy grace, that I may behave myself this day as I ought to do in Thy presence, and that

I may so commemorate the death and passion of Thy Son, as to partake most plentifully of the fruits of it. Through the same Jesus Christ, our Lord.

These my petitions I present to Thy Divine Majesty, by the hands of the Immaculate Virgin, Mother of my Redeemer, beseeching Thee, for her sake, to hear and answer them.

O Mary, Mother of Mercy, to thee do I flee for succour! As thou didst stand by the Cross of thy Son uniting thy prayers to His for man's redemption, so do thou come to my help now; kindle my devotion, aid me with thy mighty intercession, that I may find favour in the Divine Sight, worthily love and praise my God, and participate in the merits of thy Son. Amen.

Prayer at the Confiteor.

O blessed Trinity, one God, Father, Son, and Holy Ghost, prostrate in spirit before Thee, I here confess, in the sight of the whole court of heaven, and of all Thy faithful, my innumerable treasons against Thy divine Majesty. I have sinned, O Lord, I have sinned; I have grievously offended Thee through the whole course of my life, in thought, word, and deed, and therefore am unworthy to lift mine eyes to heaven, or so much as to name Thy sacred name; how much more am I unworthy to appear here in Thy sanctuary, and to

assist among Thine angels at these heavenly mysteries, which require so much purity, because Christ Himself is here in person both Priest and Victim! But, O my God, Thy mercies are above all Thy works, and Thou wilt not despise a contrite and humble heart; and, therefore, I here venture to come into Thy temple, and with the poor publican, I strike my breast and say, O God, be merciful to me a sinner; O God, be merciful to me a sinner; O God, be merciful to me a sinner. And I humbly hope to find this mercy which I crave, through that passion and death which is here celebrated. O Fountain of Mercy, grant this mercy to me and to all poor sinners. Amen.

A Prayer when the Priest goes up to the Altar.

O adorable Trinity, in Thy name, and in order to render Thee the homage and honour due to Thee, I assist at this most holy and august sacrifice.

O my divine Saviour, I unite my intention to that of the Priest at Thy altar, and offer Thee this precious victim of my salvation, and I beseech Thee to give me the same sentiments as I should have had on Calvary if I had assisted at the bloody sacrifice of Thy passion.

Grant us, O Lord, we beseech Thee, by the merits of Thy saints whose relics are here, and of

all Thy saints, a contrite and humble heart, that we may be worthy to enter with pure minds into Holy of Holies. Through Christ our Lord. Amen.

A Prayer at the Introit.

Grant, O Lord, that we may be truly prepared for offering this great sacrifice to Thee this day; and because our sins alone can render us displeasing to Thee, therefore we cry aloud to Thee for mercy. Glory be to the Father, &c. Amen.

The Kyrie Eleison.

O Father of infinite mercy, have pity on Thy children; O Jesus, sacrificed for us, apply to us the merits of Thy precious blood; O Holy Ghost, the Sanctifier, descend into our hearts, and inflame them with Thy love.

Lord, have mercy on us.
Christ, have mercy on us.
Lord, have mercy on us.

Gloria in Excelsis.

Glory be to God on high, and on earth peace to men of good will. We praise Thee, we bless Thee, we adore Thee, we glorify Thee. We give Thee thanks, for Thy great glory, O Lord God, heavenly King, God the Father almighty. O Lord Jesus Christ, the only-begotten Son; O Lord God, Lamb of God, Son of the Father, Who takest away the sins of the world, have mercy on us. Who takest

away the sins of the world, receive our prayers. Who sittest at the right hand of the Father, have mercy on us. For Thou only art holy; Thou only art the Lord; Thou only, O Jesus Christ, together with the Holy Ghost are most high in the glory of God the Father. Amen.

A Prayer at the Collects.

O Lord, vouchsafe favourably to hear the prayers which Thy Priest offers to Thee for the Church and for me.

I earnestly beseech Thee to grant me those graces and virtues of which I have need, in order to deserve Thy love. Fill my heart with eternal gratitude for all the blessings which Thou hast conferred upon me, with a lively horror of sin, and with perfect charity towards my neighbour. Make my whole life worthy of one who is Thy child. I deserve not to be heard for my own sake, O my God, but I beseech Thy mercy through the infinite merits of Thy divine Son.

O divine Jesus, inexhaustible fountain of all good things, open to us, we beseech Thee, the interior of Thy Heart, that having entered, by pious meditation, into this august sanctuary of divine love, we may fix for ever there our hearts, as the place wherein are found the treasure, the repose, and the happiness of holy souls.

A Prayer at the Epistle.

Thou hast vouchsafed, O Lord, to teach us Thy sacred truths by the prophets and apostles, grant that we may so improve by their doctrine and examples in the love of Thy holy name, and of Thy holy law, that we may show forth by our lives whose disciples we are; that we may no longer follow the corrupt inclinations of flesh and blood, but master all our passions; that we may be ever directed by Thy light, and strengthened by Thy grace, to walk in the way of Thy commandments, and to serve Thee with pure hearts. Through our Lord Jesus Christ. Amen.

At the Gradual.

How wonderful, O Lord, is Thy name in the whole earth! I will bless thee, O Lord, at all times; Thy praise shall ever be in my mouth. Be Thou my God and Protector for ever; I will put my whole trust in Thee; O, let me never be confounded.

Cleanse my heart and my lips, O almighty God, Who didst cleanse the lips of the prophet Isaias with a burning coal; and vouchsafe, through Thy gracious mercy, so to purify me, that I may worthily attend to Thy holy Gospel. Amen.

May the Lord be in my heart and on my lips, that I may worthily, and in a becoming manner, attend to His holy Gospel. Amen.

A Prayer at the Gospel.

O Lord Jesus Christ, Who camest down from heaven to instruct us in all truth, and continuest daily to teach us by Thy holy Gospel, and the preachers of Thy Word; grant me grace, that I may not be wanting in any care necessary for being instructed in Thy saving truths. Let me be as industrious for my soul as I am for my body; that while I take pains in the affairs of this world, I may not, through stupidity or neglect, let my soul starve and perish everlastingly. Let the rules of the Gospel be the direction of my life, that I may not only know Thy will, but likewise do it; that I may observe Thy commandments, and that, resisting all the inclinations of corrupt nature, I may ever follow Thee, Who art the Way, the Truth and the Life; for thus only can I be Thy true disciple.

Thou, O Jesus, my God and my Lord, art the true light, for whose dawn the Saints of the Old Dispensation watched with longing eyes, looking to Thee for grace and salvation. Mary, the purest of Virgins, was Thy Mother. Taught of Thee and of the Holy Ghost, she was the first to know and love Thee; Thy sayings she treasured in her heart and fulfilled all Thy behests. May we know, believe, and love Thee as Mary did! Grant us this grace for her dear sake. Amen.

By the words of the Gospel, may our sins be blotted out, and may we walk as children of the light. Amen.

The Nicene Creed.

I believe in one God, the Father Almighty, Maker of heaven and earth, and of all things visible and invisible. And in one Lord Jesus Christ, the only-begotten Son of God; born of the Father, before all ages; God of God, Light of Light, true God of true God; begotten, not made; consubstantial with the Father; by whom all things were made. Who for us men and for our salvation, came down from heaven, and was incarnate by the Holy Ghost of the Virgin Mary: AND WAS MADE MAN. He was crucified also for us; suffered under Pontius Pilate, and was buried. The third day He rose again according to the Scriptures, and ascended into heaven, sitteth at the right hand of the Father, and He shall come again with glory to judge both the living and the dead; of whose kingdom there shall be no end. And I believe in the Holy Ghost, the Lord and Giver of life, who proceedeth from the Father and the Son; who, together with the Father and the Son, is adored and glorified; who spake by the prophets. And in one holy, catholic, and apostolic Church. I confess one baptism for the remission of sins. And I look for

the resurrection of the dead, and the life of the world to come. Amen.

A Prayer at the Offertory.

Accept, O eternal Father, this offering which is here made to Thee by Thy minister, in the name of all here present, and of Thy whole Church. It is as yet only bread and wine; but by a miracle of Thy power and grace, will shortly become the Body and Blood of Thy beloved Son. He is our High-Priest and our Victim. With Him and through Him we desire to approach to Thee this day, and by His hands to offer Thee this sacrifice, for Thine own honour, praise, and glory; in thanksgiving for all Thy benefits; in satisfaction for all our sins, and for obtaining conversion for all unbelievers, and mercy, grace, and salvation for all Thy faithful. And with this offering of Thine only-begotten Son, we offer ourselves to Thee, begging, that by virtue of this sacrifice we may be happily united to Thee, and that nothing in life or death may ever separate us from Thee any more. Through Jesus Christ our Lord. Amen.

O Mary, most faithful Virgin and Mother! thou didst present thy Son Jesus Christ in the Temple as the world's true ransom: by Him we have peace with God. What thanks do we not owe thee for thy heroic love to us, good Mother! This love it is which emboldens us to flee to thee, beseeching

thee not to forsake us, but to intercede for us with thy Son. Offer Him our hearts, that they may be His, and thine, alone. Offer Him our understanding, and may we have an ever deeper knowledge of Him Who is the Wisdom of the Father, and the source of all Knowledge. Offer Him our memory, that we may be ever mindful of His love. Offer Him our will, for we desire nought so much as to deny self, to glorify Jesus, and do His Will. Intercede for us, O Mother, that this our offering may be well-pleasing in His Sight, and may He grant us every blessing we stand in need of, both for soul and body. May we imitate thy fidelity, and do all to the Glory of God. Amen.

At the Preface.

Let us lift ourselves up to heaven, O my soul, and render thanks to the Lord our God. How just is it, O holy Father, and how reasonable, to glorify Thee, to give Thee thanks, at all times and in all places, as our Benefactor and our God! Through Jesus Christ, the angels and the virtues of the heavens, the Cherubim and Seraphim, emulate each other in celebrating Thy glory and singing Thy praises. May I, great God, unite my heart and voice with their celestial songs, and cry with them:

Holy, holy, holy, Lord God of Sabaoth: heaven and earth are full of Thy glory. Hosanna in the

highest. Blessed is He that cometh in the name of the Lord. Hosanna in the highest.

A Prayer at the beginning of the Canon.

O eternal and most merciful Father, behold we come to offer Thee our homage this day; we desire to adore, praise, and glorify Thee, and to give Thee thanks for Thy great glory, joining our hearts and voices with all Thy blessed in heaven, and with Thy whole Church upon earth. But acknowledging our great unworthiness and innumerable sins, for which we are heartily sorry and humbly beg Thy pardon, we dare not venture to approach Thee otherwise than in company of Thy Son, our Advocate and Mediator, Jesus Christ, Whom thou hast given us to be both our High Priest and Sacrifice. With Him, therefore, and through Him, we venture to offer Thee this sacrifice: to His most sacred intentions we desire to unite ours: and with this offering which He makes of Himself, we desire to make an offering of our whole being to Thee. With Him, and through Him, we beseech Thee to exalt Thy holy Catholic Church throughout the whole world; to maintain her in peace, unity, holiness, and truth; to have mercy on thy servant N. our chief bishop, N. our prelate, N. our Queen, and on all that truly fear Thee; on our pastor, parents, children, friends, and benefactors, &c., on all whom we have in any way scandalised, injured, or

offended, or for whom we are in any other way bound to pray; on all that are in their agony, or under violent temptations, or other necessities, corporal or spiritual : on all our enemies; and, in a word, on all poor sinners; that we may be all converted to Thee, and find mercy through Jesus Christ Thy Son; through whom we hope one day to be admitted into the company of all Thy saints and elect, whose memory we here celebrate, whose prayers we desire, and with whom we communicate in these holy mysteries.

O Mary, Mother of Mercy, aid us in this solemn moment, now that the light of the Great Sacrifice begins to tremble on the Altar. Ask Jesus to give us grace to love Him in this Holy Sacrifice, that we may be worthy to join our voices to those of the Angelic Choirs, and love and praise Him to our lives' end. Amen.

Consecration.

Hail most sacred Flesh of Christ, the Virgin-born! Thou art my Lord and my God, have mercy on me; I adore Thee here present under the form of bread. Eternal Truth, in Thee I believe, strengthen Thou my faith, that I may love Thee ever more and more, and hereafter behold Thee face to face in Thy Celestial Kingdom; for Thou art my heart's sole desire, my Jesus and my all.

At the Elevation of the Chalice.

Hail, Holy Blood, flowing from my Saviour's

heart, do Thou cleanse me from all sin; refresh and strengthen my soul; and preserve me to everlasting life.

Create in me a clean heart, O Jesus, and renew a right spirit within me.

Cast me not away from Thy Presence, and take not Thy Holy Spirit from me.

Give me the joy of Thy Salvation and strengthen me with Thy free Spirit.

A prayer at the Commemoration of the Dead.

I offer Thee again, O Lord, this holy sacrifice of the Body and Blood of thy only Son, in behalf of the faithful departed, and in particular for the souls of [*here name those you wish to pray for*], my parents [if dead], relatives, benefactors, neighbours, &c. Likewise of such as I have any ways injured, or been the occasion of their sins; of such as have injured me, and been my enemies; of such as die in war, or have none to pray for them. To these, O Lord, and to all that rest in Christ, grant we beseech Thee, a place of refreshment, light, and peace. Through the same Christ our Lord. Amen.

A Prayer at the Nobis quoque peccatoribus.

We humbly implore Thy mercy, O Lord, for ourselves also; we beg pardon for all our sins; we desire to detest them, and to renounce them for ever. Hoping in the multitude of Thy tender

mercies, we beg that Thou wouldst vouchsafe to grant us some part and fellowship with Thy holy apostles and martyrs, and with all Thy saints; into whose company we beseech Thee to admit us, not considering our merit, but freely. pardoning our offences. This we confidently expect through the merits of Thy Son Jesus Christ our Lord.

By Whom, O Lord, Thou dost always create, sanctify, quicken, bless, and give us all these good things. Through Him, and with Him, and in Him is to Thee, God the Father almighty, in the unity of the Holy Ghost, all honour and glory for ever and ever. Amen.

Act of Spiritual Communion for those who do not communicate.

O my sweet Saviour Jesus Christ, Thou art my sovereign good, the fountain of all good, my God, and my all. I most firmly believe that for us sinners, and for our salvation, Thou wast pleased to come down from heaven, to take upon Thee, by the mystery of Thine incarnation, our human nature, and to become one of us, that so Thou mightest be our High Priest and Victim. I most firmly believe that Thou offeredst Thyself upon the cross a sacrifice for us all, after having suffered many cruel torments for us; and that, by Thy glorious resurrection and admirable ascension, Thou hast opened the gates of heaven for us. I most firmly

believe, that in these sacred mysteries Thou art truly and really present, and that Thy sacred Body and Blood are here offered up in sacrifice, and verily and indeed received by the faithful in remembrance of Thy death. O come to me, dear Lord, in spirit, and take full possession of my heart and of my soul. To Thee I give my memory that Thou mayest always dwell in my thoughts, my understanding that it may be ever engaged in contemplating Thy love and goodness, and my will that Thou mayest direct it to the keeping of Thy holy law. To Thee I give my whole self, O my Jesus; make me to be ever Thine. May the virtue of Thy divine Sacrament increase my faith, fortify my hope, purify my charity, and fill my heart with Thy love. O let me be Thine and Thou mine from henceforth and for ever; and grant that nothing in life or death may ever separate me from Thee any more! Amen.

Dear Mother, thou who wast found worthy to be the Mother of our Redeemer, of Him Who now lies on this Altar under the appearance of Bread and Wine, help us to adore thy Son. Thank Him for us, and by the fervour of thy love atone for our cold-heartedness. Intercede for us that we may, with thee, be partakers of that Heavenly Grace which lies hidden in the Blessed Sacrament; may our faith grow ever stronger and stronger, may we have a child-like confidence, an ardent love, true

humility, and perfect obedience, may we be without spot and pure, may we abhor all that is evil, and cling to that which is good; so that we may glorify Jesus in our lives, direct all our actions to His glory, and hereafter possess Him throughout Eternity. Amen.

A Prayer after Communion.

O most merciful God! aid Thou our weakness that by the intercession of the Blessed Mother of God, whose memory we celebrate, grant us grace to arise from the death of sin, that we may serve Thee henceforth in newness of life, through Jesus Christ our Lord. Amen.

Pour Thy grace into our hearts, that we to whom the Incarnation of Thy Son was made known by the message of an Angel, may by His Cross and Passion be brought to the glory of His Resurrection, through the same Christ our Lord. Amen.

The Gospel of St. John.

In the beginning was the Word, and the Word was with God, and the Word was God. The same was in the beginning with God. All things were made by Him; and without Him was made nothing that was made. In Him was life, and the life was the light of men; and the light shineth in darkness, and the darkness did not comprehend it. There was a man sent from God, whose name

was John. This man came for a witness, to give testimony of the light, that all men might believe through him. He was not the light; but was to give testimony of the light. That was the true light, which enlighteneth every man that cometh into this world. He was in the world, and the world was made by Him, and the world knew Him not. He came unto His own, and His own received Him not. But to as many as received Him, he gave power to be made the sons of God; to them that believe in His name; who are born, not of blood, nor of the will of the flesh, nor of the will of man, but of God. And *the Word was made flesh*, and dwelt among us, and we saw His glory, the glory, as it were, of the only begotten of the Father, full of grace and truth.

O Mary, my refuge and my consolation! thank God for the blessing I have now received, and obtain for me grace to remain faithful unto death. Show thyself my Mother, and commend me to Jesus thy beloved Son, and may my sole desire ever be to praise and glorify Him. Amen.

Glory be to the Father, to the Son, and to the Holy Ghost.

Praise to her who is the Queen of Heaven and Earth, the Queen of Angels, and the Queen of Saints. Amen.

DEVOTIONS FOR CONFESSION.

Preparatory Prayer.

O GOD, Creator of Heaven and Earth and King of kings, Who hast made me out of nothing unto Thine own image and likeness, and hast redeemed me by Thine own most precious blood, whom I, a wretched sinner, am not worthy to name or invoke, I suppliantly beseech Thee to look down with pity on Thine unworthy servant. Have mercy on me, O God, who hadst mercy on Mary Magdalen, who forgavest the publican and the thief hanging on the Cross. To Thee, most loving Father, I confess my sins. Forgive me, dear Lord, for I have grievously offended Thee in thought, word, and deed. Thou didst come down from Heaven for my salvation. Thou art my Creator and my Redeemer, my Lord and my Saviour, my King and my God. Thou art my hope and my trust, my guide and my support, my comfort and my strength, my defence and my deliverance, my life, my salvation and my resurrection, my light and my desire, my help and my protection. I beg and beseech thee to assist me, and I shall be saved; direct me and defend me. Raise me up from death, for I am the work of Thy hands. Do not despise me, O Lord, for I am Thy servant and

slave, however wicked, sinful, and unworthy. If I am blind Thou canst enlighten me; if I am dead thou canst raise me to life again; because Thy mercy is greater than my iniquity; Thy loving forgiveness greater than my sinfulness. I beseech Thee, O most merciful Father, by Thy great mercy, I entreat and implore Thee to lead me to a true sorrow, a sincere confession, and an entire satisfaction for all my sins. Amen.

A prayer to obtain a full knowledge of, and a true sorrow for, our sins.

O Eternal Father, Father of mercies, and God of all Consolation, now that I am about to examine all my actions, I am filled with fear and alarm; for Thou layest open what is hidden, unlockest what is closed, and searchest the depths of the human heart. Wherefore I humbly ask of Thee to grant me that I may be able, by Thy holy grace, to remember all the sins by which I have most shamefully enslaved my soul, and to weep over them. Excite in me so deep a feeling of grief and sorrow, that I may thus deserve to obtain Thy pardon in the Sacrament of Penance.

You would here do well to have recourse to our Blessed Lady and to your Angel Guardian, by means of some short prayer; that they may assist you to prepare for this holy Sacrament worthily.

Examination of Conscience.

1. In Relation to God.

1. Have I omitted morning or evening prayer, or neglected to make my daily examination of conscience? Have I prayed negligently, and with wilful distractions.

2. Have I been negligent in the discharge of any of my religious duties? Have I taken care that those under my charge have not wanted the instructions necessary for their condition, nor time for prayer, or to prepare for the sacraments?

3. Have I spoken irreverently of God and holy things? Have I taken His name in vain, or told untruths?

4. Have I omitted my duty through human respect or interest? &c.

5. Have I been zealous for God's honour, for justice, virtue, and truth, and reproved such as act otherwise?

6. Have I resigned my will to God in troubles, necessities, sickness?

7. Have I carefully avoided all kinds of impurity, and faithfully resisted thoughts of infidelity, distrust, presumption?

2. In Relation to my Neighbour.

1. Have I disobeyed my superiors, murmured against their commands, or spoken of them contemptuously?

2. Have I been troubled, peevish, or impatient, when told of my faults, and not corrected them? Have I scorned the good advice of others, or censured their proceedings?

3. Have I offended any one by injurious words or actions, or given way to hatred, jealousy, or revenge?

4. Or lessened their reputation by any sort of detraction, or in any matter of importance?

5. Have I formed rash judgments, or spread any report, true or false, that exposed my neighbour to contempt, or made him undervalued?

6. Have I, by carrying stories backward and forward, or otherwise, created discord and misunderstanding between neighbours.

7. Have I been forward or peevish towards any one in my carriage, speech, or conversation?

8. Or taken pleasure to vex, mortify, or provoke them?

9. Have I mocked or reproached them for their corporal or spiritual imperfections?

10. Have I been excessive in reprehending those under my care, or been wanting in giving them just reproof?

11. Have I borne with their oversights and imperfections, and given them good counsel?

12. Have I been solicitous for such as are under my charge; and provided for their souls and bodies?

3. *In Relation to Myself.*

1. Have I been obstinate in following my own will, or in defending my own opinion in things either indifferent, dangerous or scandalous?

2. Have I taken pleasure in hearing myself praised, or acted from motives of vanity or human respect?

3. Have I indulged myself in too much ease and sloth, or any ways yielded to sensuality or impurity?

4. Has my conversation been edifying and moderate; or have I been froward, proud or troublesome to others?

5. Have I spent overmuch time in recreation or useless employments, and thereby omitted or put off my devotions to unseasonable times?

6. Have I yielded to intemperance, rage, impatience or jealousy?

An Act of Contrition.

O Lord Jesus Christ, lover of our souls, who, for the great love wherewith Thou hast loved us, wouldest not the death of a sinner, but rather that he should be converted and live; I grieve from the bottom of my heart that I have offended Thee, my most loving Father and Redeemer, unto Whom all sin is infinitely displeasing; Who hast so loved me that Thou didst shed Thy blood for me, and endure the bitter torments of a most cruel death.

O my God! O infinite Goodness! would that I had never offended Thee. Pardon me, O Lord Jesus, most humbly imploring Thy mercy. Have pity upon a sinner for whom Thy blood pleads before the face of the Father.

O most merciful and forgiving Lord, for the love of Thee I forgive all who have ever offended me. I firmly resolve to forsake and flee from all sins, and to avoid the occasions of them; and to confess, in bitterness of spirit, all those sins which I have committed against Thy divine goodness, and to love Thee, O my God, for Thine own sake, above all things and for ever. Grant me grace so to do, O most gracious Lord Jesus.

Prayers after Confession.

Accept, O Lord, I beseech Thee, this my confession, and mercifully pardon all my deficiencies, that, according to the greatness of Thy mercy, I may be fully and perfectly absolved in heaven; who livest and reignest with the Father and the Holy Ghost, &c.

A Thanksgiving after Confession.

I return unto Thee, O Lord Jesus, and give Thee thanks that Thou hast been pleased to cleanse me from the foul leprosy of my sins. Blessed be Thy name, O Lord, for ever and ever. Truly Thou art a Saviour who rejectest none that come unto Thee seriously desiring to repent, but receivest them

into Thy favour, and numberest them with Thy children. I acknowledge and adore Thy mercy, and dedicate myself wholly to Thy service hereafter. Assist my weakness, and suffer me not again to fall into my past sins and to be separated from Thee; but so bind my heart and soul to Thee with the cords of Thy love, that I may say with the Apostle, " Who shall separate me from the love of Christ ? "

DEVOTIONS FOR COMMUNION.

Direct your Intention.

LORD Jesus, King of everlasting glory, behold I desire to come to Thee this day, and to receive Thy Body and Blood in this Heavenly Sacrament, for Thy honour and glory, and the good of my soul. I desire to receive Thee, because it is Thy desire, and Thou hast so ordained: Blessed be Thy name for ever. I desire to come to Thee like Magdalen, that I may be delivered from all my evils, and embrace Thee, my only good. I desire to come to Thee, that I may be happily united to Thee, that I may henceforth abide in Thee, and Thou in me; and that nothing in life or death may ever separate me from Thee.

Commemorate the Passion of Christ.

I desire, in these holy mysteries, to commemorate, as Thou hast commanded, all thy sufferings; Thy agony and bloody sweat; Thy being betrayed and apprehended; all the reproaches and calumnies, all the scoffs and affronts, all the blows and buffets, Thou hast endured for me; Thy being scourged, crowned with thorns, and loaded with a heavy cross for my sins, and for those of the whole world; Thy crucifixion and death, together

with Thy glorious resurrection and triumphant ascension. I adore Thee, and give Thee thanks for all that Thou hast done and suffered for us; and for giving us, in the most Blessed Sacrament, this pledge of our redemption, this victim of our ransom, this body and blood which was offered for us.

Make an Act of Faith.

I most firmly believe, O Jesus, that in this Holy Sacrament Thou art present verily and indeed; that here is Thy Body and Blood, Thy soul and Thy Divinity. I believe that Thou, my Saviour, True God and True Man, art really here, with all Thy treasures; that here Thou communicatest Thyself to us, makest us partakers of the fruit of Thy passion, and givest us a pledge of eternal life. I believe there cannot be a greater happiness than to receive Thee worthily, nor a greater misery than to receive Thee unworthily. All this I most steadfastly believe, because it is what Thou hast taught us by Thy Church.

Make an Act of Contrition.

O Lord, I detest, with my whole heart, all the sins by which I have offended Thy Divine Majesty, from the first moment that I was capable of sinning to this very hour. I desire to lay them all at Thy feet, to be cancelled by Thy Precious Blood. Hear me, O Lord, by that infinite love by

which Thou hast shed Thy Blood for me. Oh, let not that blood be shed in vain! I detest my sins, because they have offended Thy infinite goodness. By Thy grace I will never commit them any more: I am sorry for them, and will be sorry for them as long as I live; and according to the best of my power, will do penance for them. Forgive me, dear Lord, for Thy mercy's sake; pardon me all that is past; and be Thou my keeper for the time to come, that I may never more offend Thee.

Make an Act of Divine Love.

O Lord Jesus, the God of my heart and the life of my soul, as the hart pants after the fountains of water, so does my soul pant after Thee, the fountain of life, and the ocean of all good. I am overjoyed at hearing the happy tidings, that I am to go into the House of the Lord; or rather, that our Lord is to come into my house, and take up His abode with me. Oh, happy moments, when I shall be admitted to the embraces of the living God, for whom my soul languishes with love! Come, Lord Jesus, and take full possession of my heart for ever! I offer it to Thee without reserve; I desire to consecrate it eternally to Thee. I love Thee with my whole soul above all things; at least, I desire so to love Thee. It is nothing less than infinite love that brings Thee to me; oh, teach me to make a suitable return of love!

Humbly beg God's Grace.

But oh, my God, Thou knowest my great poverty and misery, and that of myself I can do nothing: Thou knowest how unworthy I am of this infinite favour, and Thou alone canst make me worthy. Since Thou art so good as to invite me thus to Thyself, add this one bounty more to all the rest; to prepare me for Thyself. Cleanse my soul from its stains; clothe it with the nuptial garment of charity; adorn it with all virtues, and make it a fit abode for Thee. Drive sin and the devil far from this dwelling, which Thou art here pleased to choose for Thyself, and make me one according to Thy own heart; that this heavenly visit, which Thou designest for my salvation, may not, by my unworthiness, be perverted to my own damnation. Never let me be guilty of Thy body and blood by an unworthy communion. For the sake of this same precious blood, which Thou hast shed for me, deliver me, O Jesus, from so great an evil.

Implore the Prayers of the Blessed Virgin and of the Saints.

O all ye blessed angels and saints of God, who see Him face to face whom I here receive under these humble veils; and Thou most especially, ever-blessed Virgin, Mother of this same God and Saviour, in whose sacred womb He was conceived and borne for nine months; I most humbly beg

the assistance of your prayers and intercession, that I may in such manner receive Him here, in this place of banishment, as to be brought one day to enjoy Him with you in our true country, there to praise Him and love Him for ever.

ASPIRATIONS AFTER COMMUNION.

Behold, O Lord, I have Thee now, who hast all things. I possess Thee, who possessest all things, and who canst do all things: take off my heart, then, O my God and my All, from all other things but Thee, for in them there is nothing but vanity and affliction of spirit. Let my heart be fixed on Thee alone; let me ever repose in Thee, for in Thee is my treasure, in Thee is the sovereign truth, true happiness, and a blessed eternity.

Let my soul, O Lord, feel the sweetness of Thy presence. Let me taste how sweet Thou art, O Lord! that, being allured by Thy love, I may never more run after worldly pleasures; for Thou art the joy of my heart, and my portion for ever.

Thou art the Physician of my soul, who healest all our infirmities by Thy Sacred Blood. I am that sick man, whom Thou camest from Heaven to heal; oh, heal my soul, for I have sinned against Thee.

Thou art the Good Shepherd, who hast laid down Thy life for Thy sheep; behold, I am that sheep that was lost, and yet Thou vouchsafest to feed me with Thy Body and Blood; take me now upon Thy shoulders, to carry me home. What

canst Thou deny me, who hast given me Thyself? Guide Thou me, and I shall want nothing in the place of pasture where Thou hast put me, until Thou bringest me to the happy pastures of eternal life.

O true light, which enlightenest every man that cometh into this world, enlighten my eyes, that I may never sleep in death.

O King of Heaven and Earth, rich in mercy, behold I am poor and needy: Thou knowest what I stand most in need of; Thou alone canst assist and enrich me. Help me, O God, and out of the treasures of Thy bounty succour my needy soul.

Thou art the Lamb of God, the Lamb without spot, who takest away the sins of the world: oh take away from me, whatever may hurt me, and displease Thee, and give me what Thou knowest to be pleasing to Thee, and profitable to myself.

O my God and my All, may the sweet flame of Thy love consume my soul, that so I may die to the world for the love of Thee, who hast vouchsafed to die upon the cross for the love of me.

ACTS OF DEVOTION, PRAISE, AND THANKSGIVING, AFTER COMMUNION.

O Lord Jesus Christ, my Creator and my Redeemer, my God and my All, whence is this to me, that my Lord, and so great a Lord, whom Heaven and Earth cannot contain, should come into this poor dwelling, this house of clay of my earthly habitation. Bow down thyself, with all thy powers, O my soul, to adore the Sovereign Majesty which hath vouchsafed to come to visit thee; pay Him the best homage thou art able, as to thy first beginning, and thy last end; pour thyself forth in His presence in praises and thanksgiving; and invite all Heaven and Earth to join with thee in magnifying their Lord and thine, for His mercy and bounty to thee.

What return shall I make to Thee, O Lord, for all Thou hast done for me? Behold, when I had no being at all, Thou didst create me; and when I was gone astray, and lost in my sins, Thou didst redeem me, by dying for me. All that I have, all that I am, is Thy gift; and now, after all Thy other favours, Thou hast given me Thyself: blessed be Thy name for ever! Thou art great, O Lord, and exceedingly to be praised; great are Thy works,

and of Thy wisdom there is no end; but Thy tender mercies, Thy bounty and goodness to me, are above all Thy works: these I desire to confess and extol for ever.

Bless, then, thy Lord, O my soul, and let all that is within thee praise and magnify His name. Bless thy Lord, O my soul, and see thou never forget all that He hath done for thee. O all ye works of the Lord, bless the Lord, praise and glorify him for ever. O all ye angels of the Lord, bless the Lord, praise and glorify His Holy Name. Bless the Lord, all ye saints, and let the whole Church of Heaven and Earth join in praising and giving Him thanks for all His mercies and graces to me; and so, in some measure, supply for what is due from me. But as all this still falls short of what I owe Thee for Thy infinite love, I offer to Thee, O eternal Father, the same Son of Thine whom Thou hast given me, and His thanksgiving, which is infinite in value. Look not, then, upon my insensibility and ingratitude, but upon the face of Thy Christ, and with Him, and through Him, receive this offering of my poor self, which I desire to make to Thee.

Prayer of St. Thomas of Aquin.

I give Thee thanks, most holy Lord, Almighty Father, and eternal God, who hast deigned, not for any merits of mine, but solely through the con-

descension of Thy mercy, to satisfy me a sinner, and Thine unworthy servant, with the most precious Body and Blood of Thy Son, Jesus Christ, our Lord. I implore Thee, let not this Holy Communion be to me a condemnation unto punishment, but a saving plea unto forgiveness; let it be to me the armour of faith, and the shield of goodwill. Let it prove the emptying out of my vices, the extinction of my concupiscence and lust, the increase in me of chastity and patience, of humility and obedience, and of all virtues; a strong defence against the snares of all wicked enemies, visible and invisible; a bond of indissoluble union with Thee, the one true God, and an earnest of final perseverance. And I beseech Thee that Thou wouldst deign to conduct me a sinner to that ineffable banquet where Thou with Thy Son and the Holy Ghost art to Thy saints true light, fulness of content, everlasting joy, gladness without alloy, and perfect bliss, through Jesus Christ our Lord. Amen.

Crucifix Prayer.

Behold, O good and most sweet Jesus, I cast myself upon my knees in Thy sight, and with the most fervent desire of my soul, I pray and beseech Thee that Thou wouldst impress upon my heart lively sentiments of faith, hope, and charity, with true repentance for my sins, and a most firm

desire of amendment, whilst with deep affection and grief of soul I ponder within myself, and mentally contemplate Thy five most precious wounds; having before my eyes that which David spake of Thee, O good Jesus, in prophecy: *They have dug my hands and feet, they have numbered all my bones.* (Psalm xxi. 17.)

Plenary indulgence to be obtained by all the faithful, who, after having confessed their sins with contrition, and received the Holy Communion, shall devoutly recite this prayer before a representation of Christ crucified, and pray for the intentions of the Sovereign Pontiff.

PRAYERS TO THE BLESSED VIRGIN.

Offering by St. Aloysius.

To thee, O Holy Mary, my Sovereign Lady, to thy blessed trust and special care, and to the bosom of thy mercy, this day, and every day, and at the hour of my death, I commend myself, my soul and body: to thee I commit all my hope and all my consolation, my distresses and my miseries, my life and the end thereof, that through thy most holy intercession, and through thy merits, all my works may be directed and disposed according to thy will, and the will of thy Divine Son Jesus. Amen.

Prayer of St. Augustine.

O blessed Mary, how can we praise or bless thee as we ought for the readiness wherewith thou didst consent to come to the rescue of our lost world. Words fail us to express the gratitude we owe thee, but do thou deign to receive our thanks, faint and inadequate though they be. Receive and answer our petitions. Through thee may we find mercy, and be thou ever attentive to our supplications.

Accept our offerings; fulfil our desires; win us pardon for our sins, thou who art the sinner's only hope; and intercede for us that hereafter we may enjoy the felicity of Heaven, for none can have such influence as thou canst, who wert found worthy to be the Mother of Him who is our Redeemer and our Judge. Holy Mary, succour the children of misery, encourage the desponding, comfort the mourner, pray for our people, for the Clergy, and all orders of religious; and may all thy devout clients experience the benefits of thy succour. Compassionate the oppressed, and be gracious unto those who are still wanderers from their heavenly home. May the sight of thy own bliss move thee to intercede with God and thy Divine Son on behalf of us thy weeping weary children. Be propitious to those who flee to thee for aid, and do thou ever intercede for those whom thy Divine Son redeemed. Amen.

Prayer of St. John of Damascus.

O blessed daughter of Joachim and Ann! words fail us to praise thee aright, whose dignity is unequalled by that of any created being, for thou wast chosen to be the Mother of our Redeemer! He was flesh of thy flesh, bone of thy bone. Thou didst nourish God Himself at thy Virgin breast, and thy lips were pressed to His. O wonder past all human comprehension, and beyond the powers

of words to express! God, by whom all is foreknown and arranged from Eternity, loved thee, elected thee, and at the predestined time created thee to be the Mother of His only begotten Son, the Eternal Word. Therefore do thou, most Blessed Virgin, as a golden censer, glowing with celestial ardour, transform the noxious vapours of my heart into a sweet perfume, and out of the fulness of thy grace, impart to me purity of body and of soul. Fill me with sweet thoughts of thee, most Blessed Virgin, and may thy memory be with me ever in life, and death, and throughout a blissful eternity. Amen.

Memorare.

Remember, O most gracious Virgin Mary, that never was it known, that any one who fled to thy protection, implored thy help, and sought thy intercession, was left unaided. Inspired with this confidence, I fly unto thee, O Virgin of virgins, my Mother. To thee I come; before thee I stand, sinful and sorrowful. O Mother of the Word Incarnate, despise not my petitions, but in thy mercy hear and answer me. Amen.

Prayer of St. Bonaventura.

O Sweetest Virgin Mary! Heaven and earth are full of the wonders of thy love. As Jesus is replete with mercy to us-wards, so art thou also replete with grace and mercy to all who invoke

thy name. All generations proclaim thee blessed, for all owe their blessedness to thee! To thee do I sue for pity, rejoicing in the greatness of thy compassion. Through thee may we attain eternal bliss. Pray for us, most sweet Mother, that we may hereafter enjoy the presence of thy Divine Son, throughout all eternity. Amen.

Prayer of St. Anselm.

Full of love, my heart yearns for thee, O Blessed Virgin! Teach me how to reverence thee as I ought; may I rejoice in thee and serve thee faithfully. May my heart glow with thy love. Grant these my petitions, unworthy though I be, and fill my heart with gratitude to thee. May the measure of thy love to me be that of mine to thee. May I love, honour, and serve thee as I ought, and hereafter enjoy thy presence throughout eternity. Amen.

HYMN TO THE BLESSED VIRGIN.

Hail, Queen of Heav'n, the ocean Star,
   Guide of the wanderer here below !
Thrown on life's surge we claim thy care,
   Save us from peril and from woe.
     Mother of Christ, Star of the sea,
     Pray for the wanderer, pray for me.

O gentle, chaste, and spotless Maid,
   We sinners make our prayers through thee ;
Remind thy Son that he has paid
   The price of our iniquity.
     Virgin most pure, Star of the sea,
     Pray for the sinner, pray for me.

Sojourners in this vale of tears,
   To thee, blest Advocate, we cry ;
Pity our sorrows, calm our fears,
   And soothe with hope our misery.
     Refuge in grief, Star of the sea,
     Pray for the mourner, pray for me.

And while to him who reigns above,
   In Godhead One, in Persons Three,
The source of life, of grace, of love,
   Homage we pay on bended knee ;
     Do thou, bright Queen, Star of the sea,
     Pray for thy children, pray for me.

ST. CASIMIR'S HYMN.

Daily, daily sing to Mary,
   Sing, my soul, her praises due ;
All her feasts, her actions worship
   With the heart's devotion true.
Lost in wond'ring contemplation,
   Be her Majesty confessed ;
Call her Mother, call her Virgin,
   Happy Mother, Virgin blest.

She is mighty to deliver ;
   Call her, trust her lovingly ;
When the tempest rages round thee,
   She will calm the troubled sea.
Gifts of Heaven she has given,
   Noble lady ! to our race ;
She the Queen, who decks her subjects
   With the light of God's own grace.

Sing, my tongue, the Virgin's trophies,
   Who for us her Maker bore ;
For the curse of old inflicted,
   Peace and blessing to restore.
Sing in songs of praise unending,
   Sing the world's majestic Queen ;
Weary not, nor faint in telling
   All the gifts she gives to men.

All my senses, heart, affections,
   Strive to sound her glory forth :
Spread abroad the sweet memorials
   Of the Virgin's priceless worth.
Where the voice of music thrilling,
   Where the tongue of eloquence
That can utter hymns beseeming
   All her matchless excellence ?

All our joys do flow from Mary,
   All then join her praise to sing ;
Trembling sing the Virgin Mother,
   Mother of our Lord and King.
While we sing her awful glory,
   Far above our fancy's reach ;
Let our hearts be quick to offer
   Love the heart alone can teach.

THE ASSUMPTION.

See, to God's high temple above,
Mounts, amid angel-hymns of love,
   The mystical Ark of grace !
See aloft, on victory's throne,
Blended together, Mother and Son,
   In one eternal embrace !

All the sorrows her bosom bore,
All her pains and afflictions sore,
   At length supremely repaid ;
There she reigns on the cloudless height
Only less than the Lord of light,
   In hues immortal array'd !

There she lives, as a fount of grace,
Ever flowing for Adam's race,
   And still for ever to flow;
There, while ages on ages run,
Sweetly, sweetly, she pleads with her Son
   For us her children below!

Lady, than all the heavens more high!
More than seraph in purity
   A glance of pity incline;
Teach us to feel, teach us to know,
Teach us in life and death to show
   What treasures of grace are thine.

Look on this Isle from the azure sky
That bask'd so happy in days gone by,
   Beneath thy dove-like reign;
Fallen away from its faith of old,
O, bring it back to the Catholic fold,
   And claim thy dowry again.

No. 2.—EXCERPT FROM
BURNS & OATES' GENERAL CATALOGUE,
GRANVILLE MANSIONS,
28 ORCHARD STREET, LONDON, W.

LIVES OF THE SAINTS.

Aloysius Gonzaga (Life of St.). Edited by Edward Healy Thompson, M.A. Third edition, £0 5 0

Angela Merici (Life of St.) and the Ursulines. By Rev. B. O'Really. Cloth, gilt, . . 0 7 6

Benedict Joseph Labre (Life of St.). By Rev. W. Lloyd. See "Saints of 1882".

Bertrand (Life of St. Lewis), Friar Preacher of the Order of St. Dominic, Apostle of New Granada. By Father Bertrand Wilberforce, of the same Order. Illustrated by Cyril James Davenport, of the British Museum. 1 vol., 460 pp., . 0 7 6

Catherine of Siena (History of St.) and her Companions. By Augusta Theodosia Drane, author of "Christian Schools and Scholars," "Songs in the Night," etc. 1 vol., royal 8vo, 680 pp., cloth, gilt, ... 0 12 6

Charles Borromeo (Life of St.). Edited by Edward Healy Thompson, M.A., . . 0 3 6

Clare and Francis (Lives of Sts.). Cloth, extra gilt, ... 0 1 0

Clare of Montefalco (St.). By Rev. W. Lloyd, See "Saints of 1881",

Colette (Life of St.), the Reformer of the Three Orders of St. Francis, especially of the Poor Clares, among whom she revived the first fervour of their illustrious Founder. By Mrs. Parsons, author of "Heath-House Stories," "Afternoons with Mrs. Maitland," "Life of St. Ignatius," etc. Crown 8vo, x. 290 pp., . . . 0 6 0

Dimas (St.)., the Good Thief. By Mgr. Gaume, . 0 3 6

Dominic (Miniature Life of St.). Arranged in Readings for Nine Days, by the Rev. Bertrand Wilberforce, O.P., ... 0 0 4

Dominic (Life of St.). By Henri Dominique Lacordaire.
Elizabeth of Hungary (Life of St.). Cl., extra gilt £0 1 0
Frances of Rome (Life of St.). By Lady Georgiana Fullerton, ... 0 2 6
    Cheap edition, ... 0 1 8
Francis and Clare (Lives of Sts.). Cl., extra gilt, 0 1 0
Francis of Assisi (St.), New Life of. By Léopold de Chérancé. 8vo, . . . 0 7 6
Francis de Sales (Life of St.). To which are added Selections from the "Spirit of St. Francis". By R. Ornsby, ... 0 3 0
    Cheap edition, ... 0 1 6
Francis Xavier (Life and Letters of St.). By Rev. H. J. Coleridge, S.J. Quarterly Series. 2 vols., fourth edition, ... 0 15 0
    Popular edition, 1 vol., . . . 0 9 0
Francis Xavier (Life of St.). Cloth, . . 0 2 6
    Cheap edition, ... 0 2 0
Frederick (Life of St.). By Rev. F. G. Maples. With Portrait. Cloth, . . . 0 1 0
Frideswide (The Story of St.), Virgin Patroness of Oxford. By Francis Goldie, S.J. With woodcut, picturing the escape of the Saint from Oxford, by C. Goldie, Esq. Cl., bevelled edges, 0 3 6
Ignatius (Life of St.). By Mrs. Parsons, author of "Life of St. Colette," "Twelve Tales for the Young," etc., ... 0 2 6
    Cheap edition, ... 0 2 0
Jane Frances Fremyot de Chantal (Life of St.). By Emily Bowles. With Preface by the Rev. H. J. Coleridge, S.J. Second edition, . 0 5 6
John Baptist de Rossi (St.). By Rev. W. Llyod. See "Saints of 1881".
Lawrence of Brindisi (St.). By Rev. W. Lloyd. See "Saints of 1881".
Lioba (Life of St.). See "Life of St. Willibrord".
Lewis Bertrand (St.), Friar Preacher of the Order of St. Dominic, Apostle of New Granada. By Father Bertrand Wilberforce, of the same Order. Illustrated by Cyril James Davenport, of the British Museum. 1 vol., 460 pp., . . 0 7 6
Mary Magdalen (Life of St.). By Henri Dominique Lacordaire. Roan, gilt, . . . 0 2 0

Patrick (Life of St.), Apostle of Ireland. By Rev. W. B. Morris, of the London Oratory. Second edition, revised, cloth,	£0	4	0
Peter (St.) Story of. By W. D. S.,	0	3	6
Philip Neri (St.), Apostle of Rome. By Alfonso Capecelatro, Archbishop of Capua, sometime Superior of the Naples Oratory. Translated from the Italian, by Thomas Alder Pope, M.A., of the Oratory. With 2 engravings, 2 vols.,	0	15	0
Philip Neri (Life of St.). By Mrs. Hope, author of "Life of St. Thomas of Canterbury," "Early Martyrs," "Franciscan Martyrs in England." New edition,	0	2	0
Cheap edition,	0	1	4
Stanislas Kostka (Life of St.). By Edward Healy Thompson, M.A. Second edition,	0	5	0
Stanislas Kostka (Story of St.). With Preface by the Rev. H. J. Coleridge, S.J.,	0	3	6
Teresa (Life and Letters of St.). Vol. I. By Rev. H. J. Coleridge, S.J.,	0	7	6
Thomas of Aquin (The Life and Labours of St.). By the Rt. Rev. Archbishop Vaughan, O.S.B. Edited by Very Rev. Canon Vaughan,	0	8	6
Thomas of Canterbury (Life of St.). By Mrs. Hope, author of "Early Martyrs," "Life of St. Philip of Neri," "Franciscan Martyrs in England," etc.,	0	4	6
Thomas of Canterbury (Biographical Sketch of St.). Small 8vo, pp. 180, cloth,	0	4	0
Thomas of Hereford (Life of St.). By Fr. Lestrange,	0	6	0
Vincent de Paul (Life of St.). A new and complete Biography. By Henry Bedford, M.A. Cloth,	0	3	0
Willibrord (Life of St.). To which is added the Life of St. Lioba. Cloth,	0	3	0
Winefride (St.); or Holywell and its Pilgrims. By Miss Taylor, author of "Tyborne". Third ed., revised,	0	1	0
Xavier (St. Francis), Life of. Cloth	0	2	6
Saints of 1881; or, Sketches of Lives of Saint Clare of Montefalco, Saint Laurence of Brindisi, St. Benedict Joseph Labre, St. John Baptist de Rossi. By William Lloyd, Priest of the Diocese of Westminster. Second edition, pp. 122. Cl.,	0	1	6

		£ s. d.
Sainted Queens. Cloth, extra gilt,		0 1 0
Saints of the Working Classes. Cl., extra gilt,		0 1 0
Miniature Lives of the Saints. Edited by Father H. S. Bowden, of the London Oratory.		
New edition, 2 vols.,		0 4 0
Also in separate monthly packets,	each	0 0 4
Or the complete annual set,		0 3 6
Miniature Life of Mary. Cloth,		0 0 6
Cloth extra, with photo.,		0 1 0

INDEX OF AUTHORS.

Bedford (Henry, M.A.). See "St. Vincent de Paul".
Bowden (Rev. H. S.) of the London Oratory. See "Miniature Life of Mary," "Miniature Lives of the Saints".
Bowles (Emily). See "St. Jane Frances Frémyot de Chantal".
Chérancé (Léopold de). See "St. Francis of Assisi".
Coleridge (Rev. H. J., S.J.). See "St. Teresa," "St. Francis Xavier," "St. Jane Frances Frémyot de Chantal, "St. Stanislaus Kostka".
Drane (Augusta Theodosia). See "St. Catherine of Siena and her Companions".
Fullerton (Lady Georgiana). See "St. Frances of Rome".
Gaume (Mgr.). See "St. Dimas".
Hope (Mrs.). See "St. Thomas of Canterbury," "St. Philip Neri".
Lacordaire (Père H. D.). See "St. Dominic," "St. Mary Magdalen".
Lestrange (Fr.). See "St. Thomas of Hereford".
Lloyd (Rev. W.). See "Saints of 1881".
Maples (Rev. F. G.). See "St. Frederick".
Morris (Rev. W. B.) of the London Oratory. See "St. Patrick".
O'Reilly (Rev. B.). See "St. Angela Merici".
Ornsby (R.). See "St. Francis de Sales".
Parsons (Mrs.). See "St. Ignatius," "St. Colette".
Pope (T. Alder, M.A., of the Oratory). See "St. Philip Neri".
Taylor (Miss). See "St. Winefride".
Thompson (Edward Healy, M.A.). See "St. Aloysius Gonzaga," "St. Stanislas Kostka".
Vaughan (Rt. Rev. Archbishop, O.S.B.). See "St. Thomas of Aquin".
Ward (Mrs.). "St. Thomas of Canterbury".
Wilberforce (F. Bertrand, O.S.D.). See "St. Lewis Bertrand," St. Dominic".

No. 3.—EXCERPT FROM

BURNS & OATES' GENERAL CATALOGUE,

GRANVILLE MANSIONS,

28 ORCHARD STREET, LONDON, W.

CONTROVERSIAL AND DOCTRINAL.

Aid to Catholicity. By a Catholic Priest. Per doz. £0 0 9

Ancient Rome (Five Lectures on the City of), and her Empire over the Nations, the Divinely-sent Pioneer of the Way for the Catholic Church. By the Rev. H. Formby, 0 2 6

Anglicanism (Origin and Developments of). By the Rev. W. Waterworth, . . 0 4 6

Anglican Jurisdiction: is it valid? By the Rev. J. D. Breen (O.S.B.), . . . 0 1 0

Anglican Orders. Part I. . By the Rev. Father Gallwey, S.J., ... 0 0 4

Anglican Orders. Part II. By the Rev. Father Gallwey, S.J., . . . 0 1 0

Anglican Orders. Part III. By the Rev. Father Gallwey, S.J., . . . 0 0 8

Anglican Clergy in the Confessional. By the Rev. Father Gallwey, S.J., . . . 0 0 6

Anglican Ordinations (The Question of), discussed. By the Very Rev. Canon Estcourt, 0 14 0

Granville Mansions, 28 Orchard St., London, W.

Controversial and Doctrinal.

Anglicans (Difficulties of). By his Eminence Cardinal Newman. Two volumes:
Vol. I. Twelve Lectures, . . . £0 7 6
Vol. II. Letters to Dr. Pusey and to the Duke of Norfolk, ... 0 5 6

Anglican Prejudices against the Catholic Church. By Lady Herbert of Lea. New edition, wrapper, ... 0 1 0

Anglican Ritualism as seen by a Catholic and Foreigner. A series of Essays, with Appendix on the Present Position of the Church in France. By M. l'Abbé Martin, . . 0 8 0

Anglican Schism (Rise and Growth of the). By Nicholas Sander, D.D., sometime Fellow of of New College, Oxford. Published A.D. 1585, with a Continuation of the History by the Rev. Edward Rishton, B.A., of Brasenose College, Oxford. Translated with Introduction and Notes, by David Lewis, M.A. Full price 14s.; now offered for . . nett 0 7 0

Annis Christi Tractatus (De): sive Chronologiæ Sacræ et Profanæ inter se et cum Vaticiniis S. Scripturæ Concordia plena. Pars I. Quæstio Chronologica de Documentis Historiæ. Pars II. Quæstio Theologica præcipue de Vaticiniis et Interpretatione S. Scripturæ. Auctore Rev. H. Formby, . 0 2 0

Answers and Questions. By Rev. Fr. Anderdon (S.J.)

Apocalypse (Comparison between the History of the Church and the Prophecies of the). From the German. By Edwin de Lisle. Crown 16mo, ... 0 2 0

Apostle of Ireland and his modern Critics. By the Rev. W. B. Morris (of the Oratory), . 0 0 6

Apostleship of Suffering, or the Society of Voluntary Victims for the present necessities

Granville Mansions, 28 Orchard St., London, W.

of the Church, especially of the Catholic Nations of Europe, with a preface by Lady Herbert. By the Rev. N. J. Lyonnard,
 5s for £0 2 6

Aquin (St. Thomas of), and Ideology. By Monsignor Ferré. Translated by a Father of Charity. Cloth extra, . . . 0 2 0

Arians of the Fourth Century (The). By his Eminence Cardinal Newman, . . 0 6 0

Atheists, Freethinkers, and Sceptics (Safeguards of Divine Faith in the presence of). A series of Eight Essays chiefly addressed to men of the world engaged in their various professional and social avocations. By the Rev. H. Formby, ... 0 7 6

Authority and Anarchy, or the Bible on the Church. Second edition, . . . 0 2 0

Authority (Essays on the Church's Doctrinal), mostly reprinted from the 'Dublin Review'. By the late W. G. Ward (D.Ph.) 1 vol., cr. 8vo, 565 pp., cloth, ... 0 10 0

Beauties of the Catholic Church; or Her Festivals, Rites and Ceremonies popularly Explained. By Rev. J. Shadler, . nett 0 6 0

Belief (Catholic): Exposition of Christian Doctrine. Third edition, containing much new matter, ... 0 0 6

Believe? (What do Catholics really). By the Rev. Fr. Anderdon (S.J.), . . 0 0 1

Bible Vindicated (Philosophy of the). By the Rev. C. O'Brien. Cloth, . . . 0 5 0

Bible? (What is the). Is yours the right Book? By the Rev. Fr. Anderdon (S.J.) . . 0 0 1

Bible in the Middle Ages, with Remarks on the Libraries, Schools, and Social and Reli-

Granville Mansions, 28 Orchard St., London, W.

gious Aspects of Mediæval Europe. By
Leicester Ambrose Buckingham. 8vo, . £0 6 0

Blessed Sacrament, the Centre of Immutable Truth. By His Eminence Cardinal Manning. A new and revised edition. Cloth, . 0 1 0

Burning Questions. By William Molitor, . 0 3 0

Cathedra Petri; or, The Titles and Prerogatives of St. Peter, and of his See and Successors, as described by the Early Fathers, Ecclesiastical Writers, and Councils of the Church. With an appendix containing Notes on the History and Acts of the first four General Councils, and the Council of Sardica, in their relation to the Supremacy of the Pope. By C. F. B. Allnatt. Third edition, much enlarged, ... 0 6 0

Cathedra Petri: the Titles and Prerogatives of St. Peter, and of his See and Successors, as described by the Early Fathers, &c. By C. F. B. Allnatt. Second edition, greatly enlarged, demy 8vo, ... 0 3 0

Catholics in England (Present Position of). By His Eminence Cardinal Newman. New edition, ... 0 7 0

Catholic Belief: Exposition of Christian Doctrine. Third edition, containing much new matter, ... nett 0 0 6

Catholic Controversy. A Reply to Dr. Littledale's "Plain Reasons". By H. I. D. Ryder. 3rd edition, ... 0 2 6

Catholic Christian Instructed. By Bishop Challoner. New edition, cloth, . . 0 0 9

Catholicity, an Aid thereto. By a Catholic Priest, . . . Per doz. 0 0 9

Granville Mansions, 28 Orchard St., London, W.

Catholic Worship: a Manual of Popular Instruction on the Ceremonies and Devotions of the Church. By the late Very Rev. Canon Oakeley. Second edition, . . £0 1 0

Christendom (Formation of). By T. W. Allies, M.A. Vols. I., II., III., . each 0 12 0

Christian Missions. By T. W. Marshall. 2 vols. 8vo, ... 1 4 0

Chronologiæ Sacræ et Profanæ inter se et cum Vaticiniis S. Scripturæ Concordia plena: sive De Annis Christi Tractatus. Pars I. Quæstio Chronologica de Documentis Historiæ. Pars II. Quæstio Theologica præcipue de Vaticiniis et Interpretatione S. Scripturæ. Auctore Rev. H. Formby, . . . 0 2 0

Church and State as seen in the Formation of Christendom. By T. W. Allies, M.A. 8vo, pp. 472, cloth, ... 0 14 0
    To the Clergy, . . . nett 0 10 6

Church (Lectures on the). By His Eminence Cardinal Wiseman, ... 0 3 6

Church Union (The Faith of the English), A.D. 1878; of Clewer, A.D. 1878; of the Council of Ephesus, A.D. 431. By the Rev. Peter Gallwey (S.J.), ... 0 0 6

Church of Rome not the Great Apostasy. By C. F. B. Allnatt, ... 0 0 6

Church? (Which is the True). By C. F. B. Allnatt. Demy 8vo, ... 0 1 6

Church of the New Testament. (No. 1. Tracts for the Times). By the Hon. Colin Lindsay, 24 pp., ... 0 0 4

Clifton Tracts. 4 vols., . . . 0 10 0
    Vol. I. The Reformation, . . . 0 2 6
    II. Historical fallacies, . . . 0 2 0

Granville Mansions, 28 Orchard St., London, W.

III. Christian Doctrine,	£0	3	0
IV. Miscellaneous,	0	2	6
Selections in parts of ten each. Per part 6d to	0	1	0

(The Tracts may also be had separately. List on Application).

Communion of Saints. By the Rev. Father Lockhart. Bound, ... 0 1 6

Comparison between the History of the Church and the Prophecies of the Apocalypse. From the German. By Edwin de Lisle. Crown 16mo, ... 0 2 0

Compendium of the Philosophy of Ancient History: a Companion for the Study of Greek and Roman History, and a book to put into the hands of Sceptics and Unbelievers. By the Rev. H. Formby, . . . 0 4 6

Condemnation of Pope Honorius. An Essay republished and newly arranged from the 'Dublin Review,' with a few notes in reply to Rev. F. Willis, of Cuddesdon Theological College. By Dr. W. G. Ward. One vol., 8vo, paper cover, 64 pp. . . . 0 1 6

Confessional (Anglican Clergy in the). By the Rev. Peter Gallwey (S.J.) . . . 0 0 6

Confession to a Priest. By the Rev. Fr. Anderdon (S.J.), ... 0 0 1

Controversial Papers. Containing: I. Is Ritualism honest? II. Is there Unity in the Church of Rome? III. Answer to the Protestant Bishop of Manchester. By the Rev. Fr. Anderdon (S.J.) 1 vol., cloth, . . 0 2 0

Controversy (Catholic); a Reply to Dr. Littledale's "Plain Reasons". By the Rev. H. I. D. Ryder, "Of the Oratory". 3rd edition, 0 2 6

Controversial Tracts (a Series of); or, Manchester Dialogues. By the Rev. Thomas Harper (S.J.) In 2 parts each 6d and . 0 1 0

Granville Mansions, 28 Orchard St., London, W.

Conversion (Long Resistance and Ultimate). By Sir Charles Douglas. New edition, . £0 2 6

Creation (Simplicity of the). By W. Adolph, 0 5 0

Creation (Voice of), as a Witness to the Mind of its Divine Author. By the late Very Rev. Canon Oakeley, ... 0 1 6

Dialogues (Manchester): a Series of Controversial Tracts. By the Rev. Thomas Harper (S.J.) In 2 parts each 6d and . . 0 1 0

Difficulties of Anglicans. By His Eminence Cardinal Newman. Two volumes:
Vol. I. Twelve Lectures, . . . 0 7 6
Vol. II. Letters to Dr. Pusey and to the Duke of Norfolk, ... 0 5 6

Discussions and Arguments. 1. How to accomplish it. 2. The Antichrist of the Fathers. 3. Scripture and the Creed. 4. Tamworth Reading-Room. 5. Who's to blame? 6. An argument for Christianity. By His Eminence Cardinal Newman, . 0 6 0

Divinely-sent Pioneer of the Way for the Catholic Church. Five Lectures on the City of Ancient Rome and her Empire over the Nations. By the Rev. H. Formby, . . 0 2 6

Doctrinal Definitions. By W. G. Ward (D.Ph.), ... 0 5 6

Doctrine of Holy Indulgences. By Fr. Ambrose St. John (of the Oratory), . . 0 1 0

Doctrine of Justification. By His Eminence Cardinal Newman, ... 0 5 0

Educational Peril. By the Rt. Rev. Dr. Vaughan, Bishop of Salford,.. . . 0 0 4

Educated Classes (An Investigation into the Growing Unbelief of the). By the Rev. H. Formby, ... 0 1 6

Granville Mansions, 28 Orchard St., London, W.

	£ s. d.
Encyclical Letter of Our Holy Father Leo XIII. on St. Thomas Aquinas. Translated by Fr. Rawes, D.D., with a Preface by His Eminence Cardinal Manning,	0 1 0
England and Christendom. By His Eminence Cardinal Manning,	0 10 6
England and Rome. By the Rev. W. Waterworth,	0 4 6
English Church Union (The Faith of the), A.D. 1878; of Clewer, A.D. 1878; of the Council of Ephesus, A.D. 431. By the Rev. Peter Gallwey (S.J.),	0 0 6
Episcopate (Unity of the). By Edward Healy Thompson, M.A.,	0 4 6
Essays on Devotional and Scriptural Subjects. By W. G. Ward (D.Ph.) Reprinted from the 'Dublin Review'. Contents: 1. Catholic Devotion to our Blessed Lady; 2. Catholic Doctrine concerning our Blessed Lady; 3. Mary in the Gospels; 4. The Sacred Heart; 5. St. Paul's relations with St. Peter; 6. St. Mary Magdalen in the Gospels; 7. Father Coleridge on the Gospels; 8. Gospel Narrative of the Resurrection; 9. Father Coleridge's "Life of our Life". One vol., crown 8vo, cloth, xxxii., 467 pp.,	0 9 0
Essays on the Church's Doctrinal Authority. By W. G. Ward (D.Ph.) Mostly reprinted from the 'Dublin Review'. 1 vol., crown 8vo, 565 pp., cloth,	0 10 0
Essay on Assent. By His Eminence Cardinal Newman,	0 7 6
Essay on the Development of Christian Doctrine. By His Eminence Cardinal Newman,	0 6 0
Essays Critical and Historical. Two volumes Notes. 1. Poetry. 2. Rationalism. 3. De	

Granville Mansions, 28 Orchard St., London, W.

la Mennais. 4. Palmer on Faith and Unity. 5. St. Ignatius. 6. Prospects of the Anglican Church. 7. The Anglo-American Church. 8. Countess of Huntingdon. 9. Catholicity of the Anglican Church. 10. The Antichrist of Protestants. 11. Milman's Christianity. 12. Reformation of the Eleventh Century. 13. Private Judgment. 14. Davison. 15. Kemble. By His Eminence Cardinal Newman, ... £0 12 0

Essays on Miracles (Two). 1. Of Scripture. 2. Of Ecclesiastical History. By His Eminence Cardinal Newman, . . . 0 6 0

Eternity of Punishment of the Reprobate. By the Rev. H. Formby. Wrapper, . 0 6 3

Eutropia, or How to find a Way out of Darkness into Light. By the Rev. Pius Devine, Passionist. 1 vol., cr. 8vo, cloth, boards. 433 pp., ... 0 7 0

Faith (Safeguards of Divine), in the presence of Sceptics, Freethinkers, and Atheists. A series of Eight Essays chiefly addressed to men of the world engaged in their various professional and social avocations. By the Rev. H. Formby, ... 0 7 6

Faith of the English Church Union, A.D. 1878; of Clewer, A.D. 1878; of the Council of Ephesus, A.D. 431. By the Rev. Peter Gallwey (S.J.), ... 0 0 6

Fourfold Sovereignty of God. By His Eminence Cardinal Manning. Second edition, . 0 2 6
   Cloth, ... 0 3 6

Formation and Growth of Society out of Christian Marriage, and its connection with the Religious Orders. By the Rev. R. Belaney, M.A., Cam., ... 0 1 0

Granville Mansions, 28 Orchard St., London, W.

Controversial and Doctrinal.

Formation of Christendom. By T. W. Allies, M.A. Vols. I., II., III., each . £0 12 0

Freemasonry, Secret Warfare of. Translated from the German, with an Introduction. Crown 8vo, cloth, ... 0 5 0

Free-Will, and Miracles (Science, Prayer,). By Dr. W. G. Ward. Second edition, . 0 1 0

Gain (Loss and). By His Eminence Cardinal Newman, ... 0 5 6

Geology and Revelation. By the Rev. Gerald Molloy (D.D.) With Illustrations. New edition, ... 0 6 6

God or no God, and the Immortality of the Soul. (No. 2. Tracts for the Times). By The Hon. Colin Lindsay. 16 pp., . . 0 0 3

Grounds of Faith. By His Eminence Cardinal Manning. Cloth, ... 0 1 6

Honorius (Condemnation of Pope). An Essay republished and newly arranged from the 'Dublin Review,' with a few notes in reply to Rev. F. Willis, of Cuddesdon Theological College. By Dr. W. G. Ward. One vol., 8vo, paper cover, 64 pp., . . . 0 1 6

Honorius (Reply to Renouf on Pope). By the Rev. Father Bottalla (S.J.), . . . 0 8 6

Idea of a University. 1. Nine Discourses. 2. Occasional Lectures and Essays. By His Eminence Cardinal Newman, . . 0 7 0

Ideology (St. Thomas of Aquin and). By Monsignor Ferré. Translated by a Father of Charity. Cloth extra, . . . 0 2 0

Immortality of the Soul (God or no God, and the). Being No. 2. Tracts for the Times. By the Hon. Colin Lindsay. 16 pp., . 0 0 3

Indulgences (Doctrine of Holy). By the Rev. Fr. Ambrose St. John, of the Oratory, . 0 1 0

Granville Mansions, 28 Orchard St., London, W.

Controversial and Doctrinal.

Infallibly? (When does the Church speak). By the Rev. Fr. Knox (D.D.), of the Oratory, . £0 4 0

Infidelity (the Principal Causes of), or, Why Men do not Believe. By Mgr. N. R. Laforet, 5s for nett 0 2 6

Instructed (Catholic Christian). By the Rt. Rev. Bishop Challoner, . . . 0 0 9

Investigation into the Growing Unbelief of the Educated Classes. By the Rev. H. Formby, 0 1 6

Italy (Pope and). By A. Wood. Wrapper, . 0 1 0

Jesus Christ? (Who is). By the Rt. Rev. Dr. Hedley (O.S.B.), Bishop of Newport and Menevia 0 1 4

Jurisdiction (Anglican): is it valid? By the Rev. J. D. Breen (O.S.B.), . . . 0 1 0

Leo XIII. (Encyclical Letter of Our Holy Father), on St. Thomas Aquinas. Translated by Fr. Rawes, D.D., with a Preface by His Eminence Cardinal Manning . . . 0 1 0

Letter to his Parishioners by Hon W. Towry, late Vicar of Harborne, near Birmingham, and late Chancellor Bath and Wells. 3rd edition. Stitched, ... 0 1 0

Lion in the Path. By the Rev. Fr. Anderdon (S.J.), ... 0 0 1

Long Resistance and Ultimate Conversion. By Sir Charles Douglas. New edition, . 0 2 6

Loss and Gain. By His Eminence Cardinal Newman, ... 0 5 6

Manchester Dialogues; a Series of Controversial Tracts. By the Rev. Thomas Harper (S.J.) In 2 parts each 6d and . . 0 1 0

Marriage in Pre-Christian and Christian Dispensations. By the Rev. R. Belaney, M.A., Cam., ... 0 1 0

Granville Mansions, 28 Orchard St., London, W.

Controversial and Doctrinal.

Marriage (The Formation and Growth of Society out of Christian), and its connection with the Religious Orders. By the Rev. R. Belaney, M.A., Cam., ... £0 1 0

Marriage in this Country (Extracts from the Ecclesiastical and Civil Laws regarding). For the use of lay persons, . . . 0 0 3

Miracles (Science, Prayer, Free-Will, and). By Dr. W. G. Ward. Second edition, . . 0 1 0

Missions (Christian). By T. W. Marshall. 2 vols. 8vo, ... 1 4 0

Nature-Myth Theory untenable from the Scriptural Point of View. By Lord Arundell of Wardour. Demy 8vo, . . . 0 0 6

Non Possumus. By the Rev. Father Lockhart, 0 1 6

Old Religion (The). By the Rev. Father Lockhart, ... 0 5 0

Orders (Protestant). A Reply to the Inquiry "Are Clergymen of the English Church rightly ordained". By an English Catholic. Cloth, 0 2 0

Ordinations (The Question of Anglican) discussed. By the Very Rev. Canon Estcourt, 0 14 0

Origin and Developments of Anglicanism. By the Rev. W. Waterworth, . . 0 4 6

Papacy and Schism. By the Rev. Father Bottalla (S.J.) 0 2 6

Peace through the Truth: or Essays on Subjects connected with Dr. Pusey's 'Eirenicon.' By the Rev. Thomas Harper (S.J.),
1st Series, 8vo, ... 0 15 0
2nd Series, 8vo, ... 1 1 0

Peril (Educational). By the Rt. Rev. Dr. Vaughan, Bishop of Salford, . . 0 0 4

Petri Privilegium. By His Eminence Cardinal Manning, ... 0 10 6

Granville Mansions, 28 Orchard St., London, W.

Controversial and Doctrinal.

Philosophy of the Bible Vindicated. By the Rev. C. O'Brien. Cloth, . . . £0 5 0

Philosophy of St. Thomas. By the Rt. Rev. Mgr. H. H. O'Bryen, D.D. Wrapper, . 0 0 6

Philosophy (On Scholastic). By the Rev. Fr. Rawes (D.D., S.H.G.) Reprinted from "The Tablet," 0 0 2

Pope and Italy. By A. Wood. Wrapper, . 0 1 0

Pope Honorius (Reply to Renouf on). By the Rev. Father Bottalla (S.J.), . . 0 8 6

Pope (Temporal Power of the). By His Eminence Cardinal Manning. New edition, . 0 5 0

Prayer, Science, Free-Will, and Miracles. By Dr. W. G. Ward. Second edition, . . 0 1 0

Prejudices (Anglican) against the Catholic Church. By Lady Herbert of Lea. New edition, wrapper, ... 0 1 0

Present Position of Catholics in England. By His Eminence Cardinal Newman. New edition, ... 0 7 0

Protestant Orders, a Reply to the Inquiry "Are Clergymen of the English Church rightly ordained". By an English Catholic. Cloth, ... 0 2 0

Prove all things, hold fast that which is good, a letter to the Parishioners of Great Yarmouth on his reception into the Catholic Church. By J. G. Sutcliffe, M.A., . . . 0 0 6

Punishment of the Reprobate (Eternity of). By the Rev. H. Formby. Wrapper, . . 0 0 6

Purgatory, Treatise on. By St. Catharine of Genoa, with Preface by Cardinal Manning. Cloth, ... 0 1 0

Purgatory Surveyed; or a Particular Account of the Happy and yet Thrice Unhappy State of the Souls there. From the edition of

Granville Mansions, 28 Orchard St., London, W.

1663. Edited by the Rev. Fr. Anderdon (S.J.), ... £0 3 0

Question for High Churchmen. Reconciliation with the Roman Bishop; shall we seek it? 0 1 0

Real Presence. By Cardinal Wiseman, . 0 2 0

Reconciliation with the Roman Bishop; shall we seek it? A Question for High Churchmen, ... 0 1 0

Reformation (The). Being Vol. I., of the Clifton Tracts, ... 0 2 6

Religion (The Old). By the Rev. Father Lockhart, ... 0 5 0

Reply to Renouf on Pope Honorius. By the Rev. Father Bottalla (S.J.) . . 0 8 6

Return (My) to the Church of Christ. From the Dutch of A. Van der Hoeven, . . 0 3 6

Revealed Religion (Lectures on Science and). By Cardinal Wiseman, . . . 0 5 0

Revelation (Geology and). By the Rev. Gerald Molloy (D.D.) With Illustrations. New edition, ... 0 6 6

Rise and Growth of the Anglican Schism. By Nicholas Sander, D.D., sometime Fellow of New College, Oxford. Published A.D. 1585, with a Continuation of the History by the Rev. Edward Rishton, B.A., of Brasenose College, Oxford. Translated with Introduction and Notes, by David Lewis, M.A. Full price, 14s.; now offered for . . nett 0 7 0

Ritualism (Anglican); as seen by a Catholic and Foreigner. A series of Essays, with Appendix on the Present Position of the Church in France. By the Abbé Martin, . . 0 8 0

Ritualism honest (Is)? By the Rev. Fr. Anderdon (S.J.) New edition, fcap. 16mo, . 0 1 0

Controversial and Doctrinal. 15

	£	s	d
Ritualism; Lecture I. Intrductory. By the Rev. Peter Gallwey (S.J.),	0	0	4
Ritualism (Is the Blessing of Heaven on)? Lecture II. By the Rev. Peter Gallwey (S.J.),	0	0	4
Ritualistic Clergy (The Sanctity of the). Lecture III. By the Rev. Peter Gallwey (S.J.),	0	0	4
Ritualists Protestants or Catholics (Are)? Lecture IV. By the Rev. Peter Gallwey (S.J.) Extra size,	0	0	6
Ritualism and St. Peter's Mission as revealed in Holy Writ. Lecture V. By the Rev. Peter Gallwey (S.J.) Double size,	0	0	8
Ritualists owe Obedience to their Directors (Do)? Do the Anglican Clergy hold the Place of Christ? Lecture VI. By the Rev. Peter Gallwey (S.J.),	0	0	4
Ritualism and the Early Church. The Faith of St. Leo the Great. Lecture VII. By the Rev. Peter Gallwey (S.J.)	0	0	6
Ritualism (Standpoint of). By H. F. Nash,	0	1	0
Rome (England and). By the Rev. W. Waterworth,	0	4	6
Safeguards of Divine Faith in the presence of Sceptics, Freethinkers, and Atheists. A series of Eight Essays chiefly addressed to men of the world engaged in their various professional and social avocations. By the Rev. H. Formby,	0	7	6
Sceptics and Unbelievers (Compendium of the Philosophy of Ancient History: a Companion for the Study of Greek and Roman History, and a book to put into the hands of). By the Rev. H. Formby,	0	4	6
Scholastic Philosophy. Reprinted from "The Tablet,"	0	0	2
Science and Revealed Religion (Lectures on). By Cardinal Wiseman,	0	5	0

Granville Mansions, 28 Orchard St., London, W.

Controversial and Doctrinal.

Science, Prayer, Free-Will, and Miracles. By Dr. W. G. Ward. Second edition, . . £0 1 0

Scientific Value of Tradition: a Correspondence between Lord Arundell and Mr. E. Ryley, with a letter from Rev. H. Formby on the Christian Science of Tradition. By Lord Arundell of Wardour. Demy 8vo, . . 0 5 0

Secession or Schism? By Rev. Wm. Lockhart, ... 0 0 6

Secret Societies. By the Rev. Fr. Anderdon (S.J.), ... 0 0 2

Secret Warfare of Freemasonry. Translated from the German, with an Introduction. Crown 8vo. Cloth, ... 0 5 0

See of St. Peter. By T. W. Allies, M.A., . 0 4 6

Shemitic Origin of the Nations of Western Europe, and especially of the English, French, and Irish Branches of the Gaelic Peoples. By John Pym Yeatman (Barrister-at-Law). Post 8vo, ... 0 5 0

Simplicity of the Creation. By W. Adolph, 0 5 0

Standpoint of Ritualism. By H. F. Nash, . 0 1 0

Temporal Mission of the Holy Ghost. By His Eminence Cardinal Manning. Third edition, ... 0 8 6

Temporal Power of the Pope. By His Eminence Cardinal Manning. New edition, 0 5 0

Theological Tracts. 1. Dissertatiunculæ. 2. Doctrinal Causes of Arianism. 3. Apollinarianism. 4. St. Cyril's Formula. 5. Ordo de Tempore. 6. Douay Version of Scripture. By His Eminence Cardinal Newman, . 0 8 0

True Church? (Which is the). By C. F. B. Allnatt. Demy 8vo, ... 0 1 6

Granville Mansions, 28 Orchard St., London, W.

True Story of the Vatican Council. By His Eminence Cardinal Manning, .	£0	5	0
Unity of the Episcopate. By Edward Healy Thompson, M.A., ...	0	4	6
Unravelled Convictions; or 'My Road to Faith'. By a Convert. Cloth, . .	0	3	0
Via Media. By His Eminence Cardinal Newman. Two Volumes with Notes, . .	0	12	0
Voice of Creation as a Witness to the Mind of its Divine Author. By Canon Oakeley, .	0	1	6
What is the Bible? Is yours the Right Book? By the Rev. Fr. Anderdon (S.J.) .	0	0	1
What do Catholics really believe? By the Rev. Fr. Anderdon (S.J.), . . .	0	0	1
When does the Church speak infallibly? By the Rev. Fr. Knox, D.D. (of the Oratory),	0	4	0
Why Men do not Believe. By Mgr. N. R. Laforet, ... nett	0	2	6

INDEX OF AUTHORS.

Adolph (W.). See "Simplicity of the Creation".

Allies (T. W., M.A.). See "Formation of Christendom," "Church and State as seen in the Formation of Christendom," "See of St. Peter".

Allnatt (C. F. B.). See "Cathedra Petri," "Which is the True Church?" "The Church of Rome not the Great Apostasy".

Anderdon (Rev. Fr. S.J.). See "Controversial Papers," "Confession to a Priest," "Is Ritualism honest?" "Answers and Question," "A Lion in the Path," "Secret Societies," "What is the Bible? Is yours the

Granville Mansions, 28 Orchard St., London, W.

Right Book?" "Purgatory Surveyed," "What do Catholics really believe?"

Belaney (Rev. R., M.A., Cam.). See "Formation and Growth of Society out of Christian Marriage, and its connection with the Religious Orders," "Marriage in Pre-Christian and Christian Dispensations".

Bottalla (Father (S.J.). See "Papacy and Schism," "Reply to Renouf on Pope Honorius".

Breen (J. D., O.S.B.). See "Anglican Jurisdiction: is it valid?"

Buckingham (Leicester Ambrose). See "Bible in the Middle Ages with Remarks on the Libraries, Schools, and Social and Religious Aspects of Mediæval Europe".

Devine (Rev. Pius, Passionist). See "Eutropia, or How to find a Way out of Darkness into Light".

Douglas (Sir Charles). See "Long Resistance and Ultimate Conversion".

Estcourt (Very Rev. Canon). See "Anglican Ordinations discussed".

Ferré (Monsignor). See "St. Thomas of Aquin and Ideology".

Formby (Rev. H.). See "Eternity of Punishment of the Reprobate," "De Annis Christi Tractatus," "Safeguards of Divine Faith in the presence of Sceptics, Freethinkers, and Atheists," "Compendium of the Philosophy of Ancient History," "Ancient Rome and her Empire over the Nations," "Investigation into the Growing Unbelief of the Educated Classes".

Gallwey (Rev. Peter, S.J.). See "Ritualism," "Anglican Orders," "Anglican Clergy in the Confessional," "Faith of the English Church Union, A.D. 1878; of Clewer, A.D. 1878; of the Council of Ephesus, A.D. 431".

Harper (Rev. Thomas, S.J.). See "Manchester Dialogues; a Series of Controversial Tracts," "Peace through the Truth: or Essays on Subjects connected with Dr. Pusey's 'Eirenicon'".

Herbert (of Lea, Lady). See "Anglican Prejudices against the Catholic Church".

Hoeven (A. Van der). See "My Return to the Church of Christ".

Knox (The late Rev. T. F., D.D., of the London Oratory). See "When does the Church speak infallibly?"

Laforet (Mgr. N. R.). See "Why Men do not Believe".

Law (Hon. W.), Towry, late Vicar of Harborne, near Birmingham, and late Chancellor Bath and Wells. See "Letter to his Parishioners".

Lindsay (The Hon. Colin). See "Church of the New Testament," "God or no God, and the Immortality of the Soul".

Lisle (Edwin de.). See "Comparison between the History of the Church and the Prophecies of the Apocalypse".

Lockhart (Rev. Father). See "Communion of Saints," "Non Possumus," "The Old Religion," "Secession or Schism," "Who is the Antichrist of Prophecy".

Manning (His Eminence Cardinal). See "Blessed Sacrament, the Centre of Immutable Truth," "England and Christendom," "Grounds of Faith," "Petri Privilegium," "Temporal Mission of the Holy Ghost," "Temporal Power of the Pope," "Purgatory," "True Story of the Vatican Council".

Marshall (T. W.). See "Christian Missions".

Martin (Abbé). See "Anglican Ritualism as seen by a Catholic and Foreigner".

Molitor (William). See "Burning Questions".

Molloy (Rev. Gerald, D.D.). See "Geology and Revelation".

Morris (Rev. W. B.), of the Oratory. See "The Apostle of Ireland and his modern Critics".

Nash (H. F.). See "Standpoint of Ritualism".

Newman (His Eminence Cardinal). See "The Arians of the Fourth Century," "Difficulties of Anglicans," "Discussions and Arguments," "Doctrine of Justifica-

tion," "Essay on Assent," "Essay on the Development of Christian Doctrine," "Essays Critical and Historical," "Idea of a University," "Two Essays on Miracles," "Loss and Gain," "Present Position of Catholics in England," "Theological Tracts," "Via Media".

Oakeley (Very Rev. Canon). See "Catholic Worship," "Voice of Creation as a Witness to the Mind of its Divine Author".

O'Brien (Rev. C.). See "Philosophy of the Bible Vindicated".

O'Bryen (Mgr.) See "Philosophy of St. Thomas".

Ryder (H. I. D.), of the Oratory. See "Catholic Controversy".

Sander (Nicholas, D.D.), sometime Fellow of New College, Oxford. See "Rise and Growth of the Anglican Schism".

St. John (Fr. Ambrose). See "Doctrine of Holy Indulgences".

Sutcliffe (J. G., M.A.). See "Prove all Things".

Thompson (Edward Healy, M.A.). See "Unity of the Episcopate".

Vaughan (Rt. Rev. Dr.), Bishop of Salford. See "Educational Peril".

Ward (W. G. D.Ph.). See "Condemnation of Pope Honorius," "Doctrinal Definitions," "Essays on Devotional and Scriptural Subjects," "Essays on the Church's Doctrinal Authority," "Science, Prayer, Free Will, and Miracles".

Wardour (Lord Arundell of). See "Nature-Myth Theory untenable from the Scriptural Point of View," "Scientific Value of Tradition".

Waterworth (Rev. W.). See. "England and Rome," "Origin and Developments of Anglicanism".

Wiseman (Cardinal). See "Lectures on Science and Revealed Religion," "Lectures on the Church," "Real Presence".

Wood (A.). See "Pope and Italy".

Granville Mansions, 28 Orchard St., London, W.

www.ingramcontent.com/pod-product-compliance
Lightning Source LLC
Chambersburg PA
CBHW032113230426
43672CB00009B/1720